Dorset Smugglers' Pubs

Terry Townsend

To my wife Carol

with thanks for her continued
patience, help and support

First published in Great Britain in 2015

British Library Cataloguing-in-Publication Data
A CIP record for this title is available from the British Library

ISBN 978 0 85710 098 6

PiXZ Books
Halsgrove House, Ryelands Business Park,
Bagley Road, Wellington, Somerset TA21 9PZ
Tel: 01823 653777
Fax: 01823 216796
email: sales@halsgrove.com

An imprint of Halstar Ltd, part of the Halsgrove group of companies
Information on all Halsgrove titles is available at: www.halsgrove.com

Printed and bound in China by
Everbest Printing Co Ltd

Says the Cap'n to the Crew,
'We have slipped the Revenue,
I can see the cliffs of Dorset on the lee:
Tip the signal to the Swan,
And anchor broadside on,
And out with the kegs of Eau-de-Vie,'
Says the Cap'n:
'Out with the kegs of Eau-de-Vie.'

Says the Lander to his men,
'Get your grummets on the pin,
There's a blue light burning out at sea.
The windward anchors creep,
And the Gauger's fast asleep,
And the kegs are bobbing one, two, three,'
Says the Lander:
'The kegs are bobbing one, two, three.'

But the bold Preventive man
Primes the powder in his pan
And cries to the Posse, 'Follow me.
We will take this smuggling gang,
And those that fight shall hang
Dingle dangle from the execution tree,'
Says the Gauger:
'Dingle dangle with the weary moon to see.'

John Meade Falkner
Moonfleet

Every Dorset pub of sufficient antiquity
has its smugglers' tales to be discovered.
This is my selection.

Terry Townsend

ACKNOWLEDGEMENTS

Thanks once again to the old team for their encouragement and practical help – Adrienne Bradney-Smith and Brenda and Tony Stables

CONTENTS

Explanation.
Turnpike Roads
Rail Roads
Rivers
Canals
Boundary of Counties
SOMERSET
DEVONSHIRE
ENGLISH CHANNEL
Podimore Milton
ILCHESTER
YEOVIL
East Chinnock
CREWKERNE
Halstock
CHARD
Yarcombe
Wambrook
Stockland
Dalwood
Hawkchurch
Bettiscombe
Pilsdon
Stoke Abbas
BEAMINSTER
Broadwinsor
Rampisham
Evershot
Wraxall
Mapperton
Marshwood
Netherbury
Poorstock
Winford Eage
Wootton Fitzpaine
Whitchurch Canonicorum
AXMINSTER
COLYTON
Charmouth
Symondsbury
BRIDPORT
Allington
Walditch
Chilcombe
Askerswell
Long Bredy
Little Bredy
Puncknowle
Swyre
ABBOTSBURY
Axmouth
Beer
1
2
3
4
5
6
7
A
B
C
D

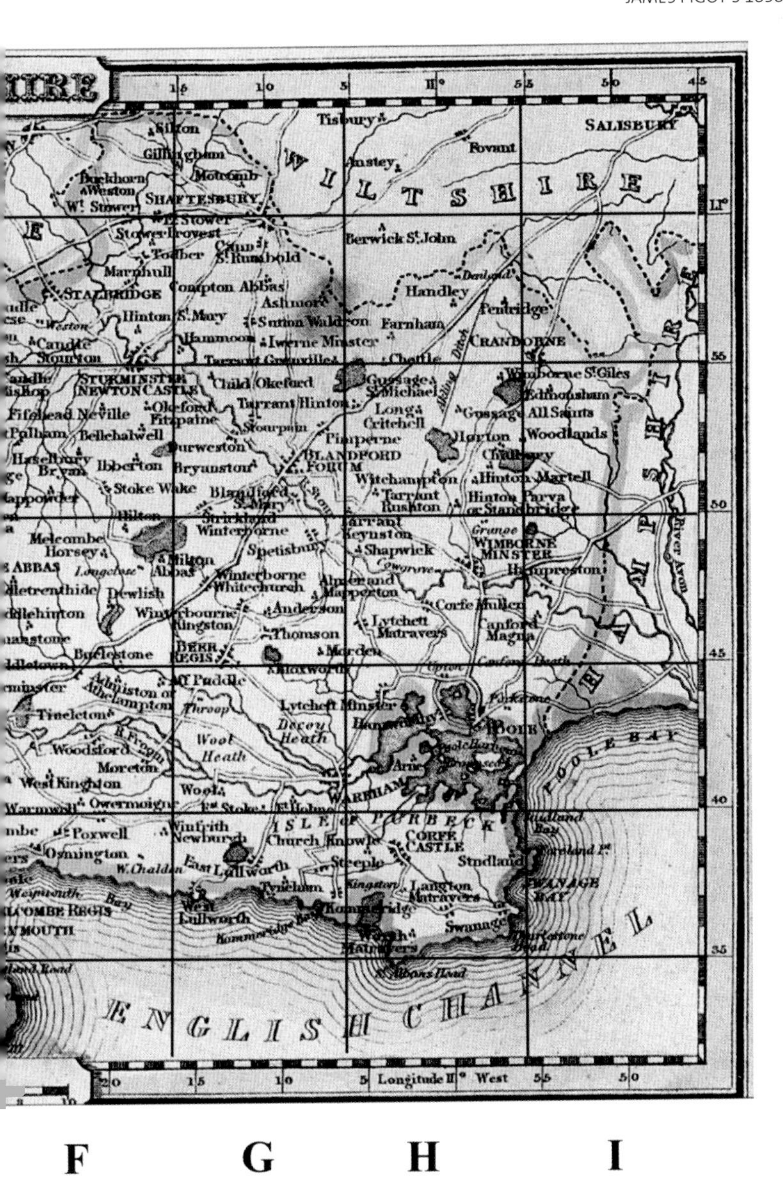

James Pigot's 1838 map of Dorset does not include Bourne Heath (present day Bournemouth) or Christchurch, which only became part of Dorset during local government restructuring in 1974. I have used the present-day county boundaries because the smuggling history of both Bournemouth and Christchurch are inextricably linked with that of Poole and other parts of East Dorset.

Inset: The Customs Riding Officers track (seen here at Swanage) is now part of Dorset's long distance coastal path.

INTRODUCTION

Few walkers today enjoying Dorset's stunning coastal path will have an awareness of its dramatic origins as a preventive measure in the fight against serious organised crime. The track was established as the nocturnal patrol route for Customs Riding Officers on the lookout for smugglers.

During the eighteenth and first half of the nineteenth centuries smuggling became a way of life in England's southern counties. During these

In 1719 it was recorded that five ships unloaded their illicit cargoes here at Worbarrow Bay.

The smugglers' pub served as a meeting place, recruitment centre, secret storage facility, distribution depot and valued customer.

politically turbulent times successive governments imposed duties on a vast range of imported luxury items to fund foreign wars. Where there are taxes there will always be attempts at evasion and so began the contest between the law and the delicious deception of smuggling.

Euphemistically termed the 'free trade', by those engaged in it, smuggling developed into a huge national industry. Sometimes up to five ships at a time were recorded unloading at selected points along the Dorset coast.

It was a logistic tour de force as thousands of gallons of spirits and hundreds of tons of tea purchased in France and the Channel Islands were shipped, landed, concealed, transported and distributed quickly and efficiently to the eager customers.

People of all walks of life were involved from the local squire to the tub carrying labourer, from the fisherman to the financing banker, from the curate to the corrupt magistrate. As Rudyard Kipling said in 'A Smuggler's Song', it was: *'Brandy for the Parson, 'Baccy for the Clerk, Laces for a lady; letters for a spy.'*

Drawing on jail records, customs reports, contemporary newspaper articles and eye witness accounts, the story of smuggling in Dorset is revealed here through the history of the pubs and inns at the heart of this enterprise.

Many of these old buildings with their low ceilinged bars, high-backed settles and inglenook fireplaces can still be found along the 86 miles of Dorset's beautiful coast from South Haven on the Hampshire border to the medieval port of Lyme Regis in the extreme west. Yet others, with their thatched roofs, flagstone floors and original oak beams made from ships' timbers are located along the network of contraband trails that led inland across the county.

Isaac Gulliver

Isaac Gulliver 1745 – 1822, the King of Dorset Smugglers.

One name mentioned more than any other in the annals of Dorset smuggling is Isaac Gulliver. The dubious deeds of this smuggling genius brought him enormous wealth and eventual respectability.

Gulliver was born at Semington in Wiltshire in 1745. Aged twenty-three he married Elizabeth Beale, daughter of Dorset publican from Thorney Down, near Sixpenny Handley, an area which abounded with smugglers, poachers and rogues of every kind.

For a time, Isaac and Elizabeth ran the Blacksmith's Arms at Thorney Down before moving nearer the coast. In later years they lived in several towns and villages in East Dorset and two of their houses – Gulliver's Farm at West Moors and Gulliver's House in West Borough, Wimborne – still carry their name.

At the height of his career, Isaac Gulliver owned properties and land extending over four counties. He invested well and widely and employed a network of contraband carriers. His army of loyal men were recognisable by the white powdered wigs they

Above left: The Blacksmith's Arms at Thorney Down, near Sixpenny Handley, which Isaac Gulliver and his wife Elizabeth ran during their early years of marriage. It is now a private house.
Above right: The White Hart, Longham, where on 12 April 1779 Isaac Gulliver offered for sale by auction twenty 'good' hack horses. The advert appeared in the *Salisbury & Winchester Journal*, coincidently with a report that the same number of horses had been seen carrying smuggled goods prior to the battle between smugglers and dragoons at Hooks Wood, near Farnham.

wore, looking more like gentlemen's servants than smugglers.

Isaac Gulliver spent his last years here at 45 West Borough, Wimborne where he died aged seventy-seven on Friday 13 September 1822.

By 1763, with the presumed partnership of Roger Ridout from Okeford Fitzpaine, Gulliver was reputed to be supplying markets as far afield as Warwick, Worcester, Oxford, Bristol and Salisbury.

Gulliver's only son died aged twenty-four but his two daughters thrived and both married well – one to a Blandford doctor, the other to a member of the wealthy Fryer banking family of Wimborne, Kinson and West Moors.

In 1782, when the British Government was desperate for men to serve in the Royal Navy it offered a pardon to all smugglers who would either enlist or find two substitutes to enlist in their stead. By this time Isaac Gulliver was a multi-millionaire and would have had no trouble in finding two men willing to join up for the right price.

Having brokered his pardon, this 'King of Dorset Smugglers' spent his last years in a large house in Wimborne becoming a pillar of the community and a Church Warden at the Minster. He died in Wimborne in 1822 and is buried in the aisle of the Minster nave between the two church wardens' seats.

Far left: Gulliver was interred in Wimborne Minster where he had been serving as a churchwarden.
Left: Gulliver was buried in the aisle of the Minster nave. His grave stone is now mounted on the wall of the west tower opposite the memorial to his only son.

BOURNE HEATH AND POOLE

The present day Haven House Inn with the original pub in the background.

Mudeford, Christchurch [Map 5I]

Haven House Inn

Haven House Inn, Mudeford Quay BH23 4AB 01425 272609

In the late eighteenth century Mudeford was a small fishing village situated at the narrow entrance to Christchurch Harbour. It is named after the little River Mude flowing out to sea here.

Negotiating the constricted 'run' into the anchorage was made doubly difficult because the sandbanks could shift overnight. To the smugglers, most of whom were superb seamen, the harbour entrance was an open gate but, to the less skilled sailors on the larger revenue cutters, it acted as a barrier they feared to pass.

On the death of her husband, Hannah Seller had taken over the Haven House Inn which stands on one promontory of the harbour entrance. In 1784 the pub played a central role in the

In 1794, at the time of the Battle of Mudeford, the near end of this building (now known as The Dutch House) was the original Haven House Inn.

largest smuggling run of the century. The drama that ensued rocked Christchurch and became known as the Battle of Mudeford.

On 15 July two smuggling luggers *Civil Usage* and *Phoenix* arrived at Mudeford Quay with a huge cargo of contraband tea and brandy. Smuggling Chief John Streeter, a Christchurch man, owned the vessels and had crewed one of them on the trip over from the Channel Islands.

Streeter had arranged for upwards of three hundred people, four hundred horses and a convoy of carts to be ready on the beach. The landing was proceeding at a pace with a beach-master directing the wagons for loading. Soon cart loads of contraband were moving slowly away from the shore bound for the heath and the forest. At that moment the cry went up as the navy sloop of war HMS *Orestes* and two Revenue cruisers were seen rounding Hengistbury Head.

Above left: The cosy bar of The Haven House. In the early days the pub extended only as far as the present day flag-stone floor area.

Above right: This serving hatch was once an opening in the exterior wall of the pub allowing thirsty fishermen to enjoy a drink without having to remove their sea boots and oil skins.

There was great consternation on the shore and John Streeter raced to the Haven House Inn for reinforcements. The luggers with their shallow draught had been beached on the shingle and the patrons of the pub got busy stripping them of all their lines and rigging.

At sea the activity was just as frenetic. Mr William Allen, the master of the *Orestes*, seeing what was happening, resolved to seize the cargo or at least, destroy the luggers. The warship and cruisers lowered six rowing boats and the armed crews pulled rapidly for the beach.

In the midst of these proceedings John Bursey, one of the corrupt Christchurch Riding Officers arrived on the scene. He was directed to a stack of over a hundred tubs which were already chalk marked as the pre-arranged bribe for his boss, Customs Supervisor Joshua Jeans.

As the preventive men neared the shore Allen shouted a warning to the smugglers ordering them to surrender. Their reply was a deafening fusillade and Allen fell back in the boat mortally wounded. Still some two hundred yards away the naval and revenue men returned fire and a running battle ensued.

The smugglers had the advantage of firing from trenches that they had dug along the beach, whereas the preventive forces, without protection of cover had to take aim from rocking open boats. When the boats finally made land the smugglers retreated to the Haven House Inn and continued firing from the windows of the pub and from nearby outhouses.

The battle continued for some hours during which the guns of the *Orestes* were trained on the pub but with the rocking of the ship some stray cannon balls actually struck the Christchurch Priory 2 miles away.

Eventually the men from the navy and revenue service captured the two luggers and a number of small boats which had been scuttled in shallow water but the price of the seizure was high. While the preventive forces were pinned down on the beach, they suffered many casualties in addition to the death of William Allen.

For the most part the smugglers melted away into the surrounding countryside. It is not known whether any of them were injured but they took with them an estimated 120,000 gallons of spirits and 25 tons of tea.

Three men were eventually arrested on a murder charge but two were released on a technicality. Only one man, George Coombes, was convicted and hanged at Execution Dock. The corpse of this luckless smuggler was hung in chains at Haven House point until sympathizers cut it down and gave him a decent burial.

In 1823 the original Haven House was taken over by the Revenue Service as a preventive station and extended to provide better accommodation. The present public house of the same name was built a little further landward along the spit.

The staff in this friendly well-run sailors' tavern are interested in its smuggling history. The old fashioned, homely little pub, with its two lovely log fires, feels like a haven, particularly on a blustery day. Well-kept local ales are from Ringwood Brewery and, as may be imagined, there is an emphasis on fish dishes on the bar meals menu.

At the back of this uniquely-sighted pub is a decking area known as the sundowner terrace where, on a summer evening at sunset, the views can be stunning.

The 'run' at the narrow harbour entrance opposite the Haven House Inn where fierce currents challenge the most experienced sailors.

The colourful mural along the front of the building clearly marks this out as a fish restaurant. The original Georgian pub, which Hannah Seller ran, is tucked behind the later Victorian street front extension.

Stanpit [Map 5I]

The Ship in Distress

66 Stanpit, Christchurch BH23 3NA Tel: 01202 485123

www.ship-in-distress.co.uk

The urban development of greater Christchurch has increased thirty times since the height of the smuggling era and the historic village of Stanpit, a mile north of Mudeford, has lost its original individual identity.

The Ship in Distress pub is located along the Stanpit Road which runs from Mudeford to Purewell Cross. Behind the buildings, and running parallel to the road, is a creek bed known as Mother Seller's Channel named after the former landlady of the Haven House Inn.

When the Coastguard Service took over the original Haven House at Mudeford, Hannah Seller moved to The Ship in Distress, next door to John Streeter's tobacco processing plant.

The oldest part of the building can be seen in the small bar to the left of the front door. Note the difference in ceiling heights. The light-hearted interior of the main bar is decorated with every nautical nick-nack from sailors' knots, brassware, lanterns and oars.

It was here that Streeter shredded and ground tobacco to make snuff. This bona fide business provided Streeter with a cover for his illegal enterprises. It also allowed him the opportunity of mixing smuggled tobacco in with legitimate duty-paid stock.

Hannah, who was deeply involved in the free trade, supported Streeter and allowed him storage in both pubs. She would also turn out her customers to assist smuggling vessels in trouble.

Following the 1784 Battle of Mudeford, John Streeter escaped detection and took refuge in the Channel Islands. However, with help from his friends and relations, he continued to run his smuggling business and his Stanpit factory. He remained under the authorities' scrutiny and in 1787, William Arnold, the collector of customs at Cowes on the Isle of Wight commented that Streeter was:

> *'Supposed to be now in the Island of Guernsey or Alderney, but occasionally [returns] to the neighbourhood of Christchurch, where Streeter narrowly escaped from being retaken by disguising himself in woman's clothes.'*

The spreading and bustling two-room restaurant area has a couple of aquariums, more fish decorations and a sail-cloth ceiling.

Although the run at the Mudeford harbour entrance was carefully guarded after 1784, plenty of contraband continued to sneak through the gap. At high tide the currents flow through the run at alarming speed, and a raft of sunken spirit tubs could be swept into the harbour right under the noses of the preventive men.

Weighted tubs were released just offshore, and often guided into the run by a strong swimmer. The incredibly fit Abe Coates (or Coakes) was possibly the last of the Mudeford smugglers to make a living as a human tugboat. Coates would ferry the tubs into Mother Seller's Channel, or even all the way to Bergman's Mill on Christchurch quay, a distance of 6 miles.

In 1804 the Government offered a general amnesty to wanted smugglers and John Streeter returned to Stanpit. Over the next twenty years he expanded his legitimate business enterprises and property holdings. On 28 October 1824 the fearless entrepreneurial smuggler ended his days in his own house next door to the Ship in Distress. Two of his children survived him. He was seventy-four years old.

The light-hearted interior of this former smugglers' pub is full of amusing seaside paraphernalia, the most eye-catching being the brightly painted fish cut-outs swimming across the walls. The pub is decorated with every nautical nick-nack from sailors' knots, brassware, lanterns, and oars, plus model boats and a statue of an old pirate.

The two-room restaurant area has a couple of aquariums and there are contemporary works by local artists for sale plus a light-hearted mural giving the impression of a window opening on to a sunny boating scene.

You are left in little doubt that this is just the place for a fresh fish dinner. Ringwood Best and a guest ale or two are on handpump alongside several wines by the glass.

On the right, now converted into two houses, is John Streeter's former tobacco processing factory. The single storey building between Streeter's business premises and the pub was probably stables and a blacksmith's shop.

Christchurch [Map 51]

Ye Olde George Inn

2a Castle St, Christchurch BH23 1DT 01202 479383

www.yeoldegeorgeinn.co.uk

Ye Olde George Inn is a Grade II listed former coaching inn located in the heart of Christchurch, a short walk away from the historic Priory Church.

Christchurch enjoys a unique location at the confluence of the Rivers Stour and Avon and on the shores of its own spectacular natural harbour. This makes it a beautiful place to visit today and rendered it a perfect location for the activities of the eighteenth and nineteenth-century free traders.

In 1776, when the vicar of Christchurch told his Parish Clerk what a grievous sin it was to smuggle, the clerk replied 'then Lord have mercy on the town of Christchurch, for who is there here who has not had a tub?'

The 1784 Battle of Mudeford focused public attention on the Christchurch smugglers, but the incident was exceptional only because of the violence of the resistance. There is little evidence to suggest that the size of the cargo landed was anything out of the ordinary.

Rev'd Richard Warner who attended school in Christchurch between 1776 and 1780 has written of his personal experience seeing smugglers at work when Christchurch Grammar School was housed in the loft above the Priory Church's Lady Chapel. Warner's Latin and Greek lessons were sometimes interrupted by the sight from his 'aerial schoolroom' as he called it, of the town's smugglers coming home from a successful landing:

Above: There is always a good representation of real ales in what was originally the 'tap' of the Piddle Brewery.

Left: The old fashioned main bar of the George has a wealth of black beams and a stone tiled floor.

'I have myself more than once seen a procession of twenty or thirty wagons, loaded with kegs of spirits, an armed man sitting at the front and tail of each, and surrounded by a troop of two or three hundred horsemen, every one carrying on his enormous saddle from two to four tubs of spirits, winding along the skirts of Hengistbury Head, on their way towards the wild country to the north-west of Christchurch.'

For some smugglers a ride in the 'Emerald' Coach to Poole was the beginning of a journey to the other side of the world.

RIght: The golden fish weathervane on Christchurch Priory tower was used as a directional warning for smugglers when preventive men were active in the vicinity.

A candle was placed in this little recess on the circular staircase of the priory to warn smugglers of the presence of preventive men.

A few hundred yards from Ye Olde George, next to the ancient bridge, is Quartleys, home of the doctor who was willing to attend wounded smugglers. A monument in the Priory Church is 'Sacred to the memory of Arthur Quartley Esq. M.D'. The last line of the inscription reads: 'Highly respected and deeply lamented by all classes of society'.

Late one night, soon after setting up his practice in Christchurch, the surgeon was woken by a loud rapping on his door. He was escorted out of town by a band of smugglers who took him to a small cottage in Bransgore, where one of their number lay severely wounded. The doctor removed a musket ball from the man's shoulder, and told his companions that he should rest and not be moved.

The wounded man who said he preferred to be moved, rather than ending his life at the end of a rope, was duly carted off deep into the New Forest (where he later recovered) whilst the learned doctor was escorted back to Christchurch. Dr Quartley's reward was a keg of brandy left anonymously on the doorstep, chalked with the legend 'Left there for the doctor's fee'.

The former schoolroom at the top of the Priory Church's Lady Chapel where schoolboys watched smugglers at work from the windows. It is now home to St Michael's Loft Museum.

Above left: The steps at 22 Castle Street where a keg of brandy would be left as a fee for Dr Quartley's services to wounded smugglers.

Above right: Joshua Jeans occupied offices in this building at 10 Bridge Street, which effectively made it the Christchurch Customs House.

A few steps further over the bridge is 10 Bridge Street, the former residence of Joshua Jeans, Supervisor and Chief Riding Officer of Customs for Christchurch. He had four officers under him and throughout his jurisdiction the smugglers had an easy time.

Jeans was totally corrupt. He encouraged his men to keep fraudulent journals and came to an arrangement with the principal smugglers to receive a percentage of each consignment in return for turning a blind eye. He was dismissed from office in 1786.

The former Eight Bells pub at 16 Church Street, which was once a haunt of smugglers, is now a gift shop. Like the George, it is said to have had tunnels leading to the Priory. According to Christchurch legends, revenue officers made a fruitless search of the inn one day whilst Kate Preston, the landlord's wife was present. During the raid she sat quietly nursing her baby while concealing a brandy tub under her voluminous petticoats.

Ye Olde George Inn is a Grade II listed pub located in the heart of Christchurch, a short walk away from the historic Priory Church. This bustling cheerful old-fashioned two-bar low-beamed hostelry was first referred to in 1630 as 'St George'.

For over a hundred and fifty years, from 1700 onwards, the majority of its patrons would have been smugglers. Later called the George and Dragon it served as a coaching inn where the Emerald Coach would stop on its way from Lymington to Poole. The old timber-framed building was refaced with brick in the early eighteenth century and some of the glazing dates back to the nineteenth century.

There are dark wooden beams and a stone floor in the main bar area. At the front of the pub is small comfortable dining room with windows looking out on the market place street scene. The paved courtyard, accessible through the coaching arch, has outdoor seating and heaters.

The pub is owned by the Dorset Piddle Brewery Company based at Piddlehinton near Dorchester. The George was originally the tap for the brewery and as such you can find a good selection of their beers plus a couple of quality guest ales.

Christchurch enjoys a unique location at the confluence of the Rivers Stour and Avon and on the shores of its own spectacular natural harbour rendering it a perfect location for the activities of the free traders.

Bournemouth [Map 5I]

The Royal Exeter Hotel

Exeter Road, Bournemouth, Dorset BH2 5AG Tel: 01202 438000

In 1800 Bournemouth as such did not exist. The historic maritime towns of Christchurch and Poole were a fraction of the size they are today and the area between was wild, uninhabited heathland where only smugglers and turf-cutters plied their trade.

Halfway along the track that linked the two ports was a wayside pub originally called The Tapps Arms, after Sir George Tapps, Lord of the Manor of Christchurch, who owned the vast majority of land now occupied by the present-day town.

The only other building was Decoy Pond House which stood in what is now known as The Square, where Debenhams department store stands today. This old cottage had long been

The Royal Exeter Hotel which incorporates Lewis Tregonwell's Bournemouth summer residence where building began in 1810 and was completed in 1812.

frequented by smugglers who landed their cargoes of spirits, wine, tea and tobacco on the beach, often quite openly in daylight.

The 1812 Lounge Bar and Restaurant of the Royal Exeter Hotel is the nearest thing to a smugglers' pub that Bournemouth has to offer.

It is well known that members of the gentry colluded in funding and organising smuggling activities. From a discovery made in 1930, and reported in *The Times*, suspicion has fallen on Lewis Tregonwell, who for many years was revered as 'The Founder' of Bournemouth.

Lewis Dymoke Grosvenor Tregonwell was born in Anderson, Dorset in 1758. At the age of twenty-three he married Katherine Sydenham, a considerable heiress. By 1787 he had spent Katherine's inheritance and the couple escaped to France ahead of their creditors. Tregonwell later extorted money from his feeble-minded father-in-law and used it to buy Cranborne Lodge.

Katherine died in 1794 and Lewis married Henrietta Portman, daughter of wealthy Henry Portman of Bryanston. Letting Anderson Manor to tenants, Tregonwell lived in style with his new wife at Cranborne. Whilst there he acquired a servant (sometimes referred to as his butler) who was a member of the Symes smuggling clan of Cranborne, Verwood and Sixpenny Handley.

The full portrait of Captain L. D. G. Tregonwell known as 'the founder of Bournemouth', can be seen in the Mayor's Parlour in Bournemouth Town Hall.

Henrietta suffered an illness at Cranborne Lodge and Tregonwell took her to Mudeford for a holiday. This whole area was one that he had come to know well when he had been Coast Commander of the Dorset Rangers between 1796 and 1802 at the time of Napoleon's threatened invasion of England. Part of his duties was to support the Preventive Service.

One day, during their holiday, the Tregonwells rode across the heath where he had formerly led his patrols until they reached a stream (The Bourne) which cut through one of the valleys, known here as Chines or Bunnies.

Tradition has it that Henrietta fell in love with the area and her husband built a summer residence here. Tregonwell paid Sir George Tapps £179 and 11 shillings for 8½ acres west of the Bourne stream – land then considered to be nothing but worthless heathland. The house is now a wing of the Royal Exeter Hotel but at the time their only neighbours would have been gypsies.

Behind sealed off doors in the basement of the Royal Exeter are tunnel entrances. One tunnel from the present kitchen area led directly to the beach.

Encouraged by the Tregonwell's lead, other wealthy people began to build villas and gradually the wasteland of Bourne Heath developed into the town of Bournemouth.

Although Thomas Symes, (sometimes spelt Sims) never appeared to travel with Tregonwell, his master built him a very smart thatched house near to his own which was named Portman Lodge.

Suspicions were raised in 1930 when the lodge was demolished and a secret underground cellar was discovered. The Times reported that the chamber was 3 feet below the ground surface, with an arched roof 6 feet above the floor. It was 10 feet long and 7 feet wide and was accessible through a trapdoor.

Looking at Bournemouth today, especially during the height of the holiday season, it is difficult to imagine smugglers' boats landing here on the then deserted beach, or contraband cargoes being openly transported inland along the chines and up through what is now the commercial heart of the town. However, numerous references to such activities appear in the journals of Customs Riding Officers.

In 1810 Tregonwell built the impressive Portman Lodge for smuggler Thomas Symes, who was supposedly his butler. It was here, during demolition in 1930 that a secret cellar was discovered.

In 1812 Tregonwell remodelled or rebuilt the Tapps Arms and renamed it the Tregonwell Arms. It later became a Temperance Coffee Tavern before finally being demolished in 1885.

One report from 1787 tells of a smugglers' lugger unloading brandy and tea near where Bournemouth Pier stands today. The smugglers were spotted by a Revenue cutter and ran off when an armed party was sent ashore. However, they

This nineteenth-century illustration of the beach at Bournemouth shows how perfect the terrain was for smugglers. They could beach their boats at the foot of the cliffs and use the gulleys as temporary hiding places before moving the contraband inland through the chines.

returned to reclaim their goods and this time they had many more armed and mounted colleagues. A terrific fire-fight ensued in which there were casualties on both sides before the smugglers regained their cargo. The leader of the revenue men was savagely beaten. Eventually the gang leader was caught, convicted and hanged at Newgate Prison.

In 1832 Tregonwell died at the age of seventy-three and was buried in Anderson but in 1843 his widow had his remains transferred to a vault in St Peter's churchyard at Bournemouth. Following the 1930 discovery, subsequent mayors of Bournemouth dropped the practice of laying a wreath on Tregonwell's tomb at the annual anniversary of his death.

This painting called 'Smugglers at Bourne Mouth' is thought to depict the King of Dorset Smugglers, Issac Gulliver and his men taking a break following a successful landing. The picture hung in the Tregonwell Arms until the pub's demolition in 1885.

The portrait of Lewis Tregonwell can be seen in the Mayor's Parlour in

Bournemouth Town Hall and there is a statue of him across the road from the Royal Exeter.

The hotel bar is located in a new extension of what was formerly the Tregonwells' summer residence. Known locally as the Mansion, the house, which now forms part of the Royal Exeter Hotel, was occupied by the Tregonwells from 24 April 1812.

The 1812 Lounge Bar and Restaurant of the Royal Exeter Hotel is not strictly speaking a 'smugglers' pub' but it is the nearest thing to it that Bournemouth can offer. It is the sort of up-market place where you might more likely be expected to order a cocktail but they do serve a pint of real ale and are aware of the smuggling history.

Bournemouth seen in the distance from Hengistbury Head shows how all the coastline between Christchurch and Poole would have looked in smuggling days.

Today the Bourne Stream flows through the landscaped pleasure gardens which were originally part of the grounds of Tregonwell's House.

The King's Head is the second oldest pub in Poole, the oldest is The Antelope which stands next door on the right hand side. Scaplen's Court, the town's most intact medieval domestic building is on the left.

Poole [Map 5H]

The King's Head

6 High Street BH151BP Tel: 01202 681150

The ancient maritime town of Poole lies 5 miles west of Bournemouth and is situated on the north shore of Poole Harbour. At its peak in the eighteenth century Poole was one of the busiest ports in Britain.

Covering an area of approximately 14 square miles, Poole Harbour is one of the largest natural harbours in the world. The area was perfect for smugglers with its dozens of creeks and inlets plus the many roads and tracks leading from the beaches across the barren heathland.

Smuggling long played a role in Poole with the most notorious incident being a raid in 1747 by the Hawkhurst Gang who successfully reclaimed tea and brandy impounded in the King's Cellars on Poole Quay, now Poole Museum, whose entrance is just a couple of steps from the King's Head.

Right: Plaster on the wall in the bar is being removed to reveal the original medieval stone work.

Far right: In 1954 this void in the wall was discovered and found to conceal remains of a spiral passageway which led from the bar to first floor.

Above left: The back area of the bar has this original square pattern plaster-enriched sixteenth-century ceiling.

Above right: The roof timbers of the King's Head are still the originals and are the same pattern of those next door in Scaplen's Court. They can be seen during August when the Court is open to the public. In school time the Court is used as Poole Museum's learning centre. The gardens are open from May to September.

An investigation into the operation of the Poole Customs House in the late seventeenth century revealed many abuses and named John Carter as one of the key operators in the area.

As well as being a notorious smuggler, Carter also traded as a legitimate merchant.

His usual technique for landing illicit goods was to arrange for his ships to hover a little way off shore where they could unload the contraband into shallow-draught 'dragger boats', used by oyster fishers.

Once the goods were ashore Carter's businesses provided a variety of storage and hiding places for concealing the contraband. These included a windmill, a malthouse, a brewery, a shop, various stables, cellars, barley lofts and wood yards. Carter and his men also stored goods at the King's Head pub which they used as their headquarters.

When Carter's gang travelled through Poole, they wore masks and women's tall hats. In this bizarre but effective disguise they were unrecognizable and the sight of the substantial clubs they carried deterred any would be informers. In 1678 the Customs Collector for Poole was dismissed for fraud whilst collaborating with Carter's gang.

Brownsea Island in Poole Harbour, seen here from the beach at Poole Quay. An additional Customs House was established on Brownsea to help combat smuggling.

The Customs House on Poole Quay built in 1813 with its replica of the town beam used for weighing goods.

In the days when Carter and his men were frequenting the pub it was called the Plume of Feathers. By the time Isaac Gulliver came on the scene a hundred years later the name had been changed to the King's Head. At one point in his career the bounty on Gulliver was worth more than a landsman's yearly wage and he had to be mindful of this when making business calls on his clients in the various inns and taverns in Poole.

One day he had news the revenue men were searching for him along the quay. He took refuge in the King's Head with his friend Mr Martin, the landlord, who helped arrange his escape back to the safety of his home at Kinson.

The King's Head is the second oldest public house in Poole after The Antelope, which stands next door. The pub was built, or rebuilt, sometime in the fifteenth century and the 2 feet thick front wall was re-faced in brick in the eighteenth-century.

In 1877 the pub was purchased by Hall & Woodhouse. Over

the years they remodelled and refitted the interior many times masking most of its medieval features. The roof timbers are still original and are of the same pattern as those in Scaplen's Court next door.

In 1954, when building work was taking place, a void was found in the wall of one of the rear rooms. It was at first believed to be a Priest Hole, but was later found to be the remains of a spiral passageway leading to the first floor.

The present day nondescript open plan bar stretches the full width of the building. A large wallpaper mural of books on bookshelves covers the right-hand wall. On the left hand wall, above a bricked-in fireplace, some of the plaster has been removed to reveal a section of the original stone. As I write there are plans for revealing more of the stonework, opening up the fireplace and installing a log-basket fire and making a feature of the secret alcove.

The building to the left of the King's Head is Scaplen's Court; one of four buildings comprising Poole Museum. The spectacular roof timbers are similar to those in the King's Head. The main building of Poole Museum, with its smuggling artefacts and displays, stands obliquely opposite the pub.

The King's Head stands a few paces from the excellent Poole Museum. Among the exhibits are displays of the town's smuggling history with a number of artefacts including this pistol, powder flask, powder measure and lead shot used by Poole smugglers in the eighteenth or nineteenth-centuries.

Kinson [Map 4I]

Gulliver's Tavern

1492 Wimborne Road, Bournemouth BH11 9AD 01202 580739

The parish of Kinson is on the south bank of the River Stour 7 miles north of the smugglers' beaches at Bournemouth. Today this formerly notorious place is a busy suburb of the Bournemouth conurbation but there are still areas preserved as nature reserves.

During the smuggling era Kinson was a separate very rural village and Roger Gutteridge in *Dorset Smugglers* says: 'There is no Dorset village with stronger smuggling connections than Kinson'.

Isaac Gulliver (1745-1822) has long been recognised as a smuggling genius whose dubious deeds brought him great wealth and eventual respectability. The village, originally known as Kingston was at the heart of Gulliver's territory and he created a track for transporting contraband from Branksome Chine to Kinson through Talbot Woods via 'Pug's Hole'.

The man who became known as 'The King of Smugglers' owned a substantial amount of property in and around the

This early photograph shows the Dolphin Inn, fronting the unmade road much as Isaac Gulliver would have known it.

Kinson area. Once landed goods reached the village there was a myriad of available hiding places including Gulliver's own house, Howe Lodge, which he had built with that purpose in mind.

After a refit in the 1980s, the pub was renamed Gullivers Tavern.

When the Lodge was demolished in the 1950s it still contained a secret entrance leading to a small room about 10 feet up the chimney which was impossible to see from the fireplace. There was also a trap door leading to a secret cellar as well as several tunnels.

The parish church of St Andrew's in Millhams Road is the oldest church in Bournemouth. It is known as the 'smuggler's church' because of the role it played in the free traders' activities. The tower acted as a lookout point and meeting place and the belfry was used as a contraband store. Over decades, ropes used to haul up goods cut deep grooves into the soft stone of the door arch inside the tower which can still be seen today.

There is documented evidence to confirm that a number of churches were used as contraband warehouses and repeated

Above left: The large main bar has recessed seating areas and a games room.
Above right: This heavily beamed ceiling which Gulliver would have known is made in part from ships' timbers.

The grave of smuggler Robert Trotman, barbarously murdered on the shore near Poole by sailors from a Royal Navy cutter.

claims that table top tombs, like the Oakley family tomb in Kinson, were used for hiding kegs.

Many of the graves in St Andrew's churchyard can be linked to smugglers, the most well-known being that of Robert Trotman who died in 1765 in the crossfire of an ambush on the sands at Poole as he loaded tea onto the waiting horses. His gravestone bears the words of a bitter community completely embroiled in the smuggling trade: 'To the memory of Robert Trotman, who was barbarously murdered on the shore near Poole'.

The tower of St Andrew's served as a lookout point, and the belfry as a contraband store. Deep rope marks can still be seen cut in the soft stone of the parapet and door arch inside the tower.

The authorities were well aware of Gulliver's activities and in 1782 they raided a granary that stood near the pub. They seized 416 galls of brandy, 50 galls rum, 458 galls of Geneva gin, 56 lbs of coffee and 5,594 lbs of tea. There were also 4 pipes of wine (420 galls), duty unpaid, belonging to Isaac Gulliver who was by then trading legitimately as a wine merchant to mask his illegal pursuits.

A raid on 19 February, a couple of years later by forty navy men in the service of the Port of Poole was a disaster. Word had preceded them and the sailors were met by a force of a hundred smugglers. As the preventives began their search the smugglers launched an attack.

The sailors returned alive but empty handed to Poole. They were treated by the surgeon and twenty seven were confined to 'sick quarters'. Although some were badly injured it was Gulliver's lifelong claim that he 'never killed a king's man'. Sixty years after Trotman's death, Henry Tiller was buried in this churchyard. He was convicted of smuggling in 1826 and, as he was unable to pay the £100 fine, he spent ten months in Dorchester jail. Tiller was known for collecting kegs of brandy

Claims have been made that this table top tomb near the door of the church was used as a contraband store.

from the seashore and running all the way to Kinson Church with them in a wheelbarrow.

Gulliver's Tavern existed before 1758 as an alehouse called the 'Dolphin & Chequer' which was later shortened to The Dolphin Inn. In Gulliver's time the pub was run by John Potter and his wife Hannah. During the 1784 raid some of the battling smugglers had been recognised and named in an official report. Among those on the list was Hannah Potter.

After a refit in the 1980s, the present building was named Gulliver's Tavern in tribute to the village's most infamous resident. Today the pub remains an integral part of the Kinson community. It is a no nonsense boozer, as far removed from a gastro pub as possible to imagine. When I enquired there about the smuggling history the friendly landlady gave me a copy of a map showing Gulliver's local smuggling locations. It is also: *A self-guided trail celebrating North Bournemouth's history and wildlife* published by Bournemouth Borough Council.

Gulliver's Tavern has one large straight bar with recessed seating areas plus a games room. The oldest room in the pub is quite a surprise. It can be dated to 1750 and has boarded walls and a low sunken timber ceiling supported by heavy beams made in part from ships' timbers.

The former smugglers' trail through the present day 'Pug's Hole' Nature Reserve.

NORTH AND EAST DORSET

Almer [Map 4G]

The Worlds End

Worlds End, Nr Blandford Forum DT11 9EW Tel: 01929 459 671

www.worldsendalmer.co.uk

In October 1770 a band of smugglers with forty fully laden horses were tracked here to The Worlds End pub at Almer.

Almer is a small parish in the Blandford district of Dorset, located on the A31 road near Winterborne Zelston. The army camp at Blandford, now home to the Royal Signals, was established in 1724 when a troop of Hussars was stationed in the area for anti-smuggling duties. These duties were later taken over by Dragoons.

Blandford's proximity to known smuggling routes was one

The original bar at The Worlds End much as the smugglers would have known it.

Exposed beams and a pleasing mix of furnishing styles present a welcoming feel to the interior.

of the main reasons why troops were stationed here from time to time during the eighteenth century.

In 1756, to counter the threat of a French invasion during the Seven Years War, an army of 10,000 men was established and major exercises were held on Blandford Downs on the site of the present-day camp.

In October 1770, Richard Cole, the Customs Waiter and Searcher at Wareham and his colleague, Riding Officer Mr Belcher, tracked a gang of smugglers from the Isle of Purbeck to The Worlds End pub at Almer.

Cole had received word that forty fully laden horses had passed over Holme Bridge between Lulworth and Wareham. He and Belcher tracked the hoof-prints all the way to The Worlds End pub on the Wimborne to Bere Regis road.

When they arrived they saw provisions laid out for 'a great number of people'. The landlord, not surprisingly, refused to stable the Custom men's horses. With no way of being able to carry off contraband, should they find any in a search, the officers agreed to split up. Belcher rode off to Poole to fetch reinforcements from the Custom House while Cole headed for Blandford and the troop of Dragoons quartered there.

The feature fireplaces have had a recent spruce up.

The army seemed reluctant to become involved in these domestic incidents probably because the Custom men were not happy to share their reward for seizures so Cole consequently had a poor reception. The commanding officer, Colonel Hay said 'he had no orders to let any of his men go'. Belcher fared no better. The Poole reinforcements took so long in 'furnishing themselves with horses' that by the time they arrived at The Worlds End the smugglers had been refreshed and were long gone taking their contraband with them.

This handsome thatched family dining pub is owned by Blandford brewers Hall & Woodhouse. There are panelled alcoves off the very long open plan busy bar and picnic sets with heaters in front of the pub plus a children's play area.

In 1724 a troop of Hussars was stationed in the area for anti-smuggling duties. These duties were later taken over by Dragoons.

In 1992 there was a disastrous fire here and the pub you see today was rebuilt in the image of the original. As I write, The Worlds End has just undergone a re-fit in which the exposed beams and stone flooring have been retained and the big feature fireplaces have been spruced up.

The Inn at Cranborne is the focal point of the village.

Cranborne [Map 2I]

The Inn at Cranborne

Cranborne, Wimborne BH21 5PP Tel: 01725 551249

www.theinnatcranborne.co.uk

This charming village of red brick and cob houses on the River Crane lies 15 miles north of Bournemouth. The Manor dates back to the Middle Ages when King John was a regular visitor during his hunting trips to Cranborne Chase. Like the New Forest, and surrounding areas, Cranborne Chase became a notorious haunt of smugglers, cutpurses and other brigands. There is a record of a smuggling incident associated with Cranborne in the late eighteenth century. It features the Inn at Cranborne in the days when it was known as the 'Flower de Luce'. The tale involves a noted smuggler called Daniel Sims who was born in nearby Verwood in 1759.

Following a tip off, the Excise Officer at Cranborne, travelled to Verwood and searched Dan's premises. He discovered eleven casks of spirits 'concealed in an underground cell constructed for the purpose'. At the time Dan was out cutting turves on the common and his brother-in-law rode out to give him the bad news.

The Excise party returned home with the casks but Dan followed their trail to Cranborne and put up his horse in the stable of the Flower de Luce. The disgruntled smuggler then went into the bar and sat quietly in the chimney corner, with his pipe and glass. He soon received intelligence that his seized kegs were lodged in the Exciseman's house, which stood at the corner of the street opposite the pub.

Above left: The long main bar/dining room has a number of cosy corners.

Above right: Wood burning stoves enhance the feature fire-places.

Finishing his drink Dan rode off to arrange for the recovery of the contraband. Smuggling colleagues rallied to the call and a transport column with carts and horses arrived near Cranborne around midnight.

The gang stopped at Deadman's cross not far from the village and one of them went ahead to mark the Exciseman's door with chalk, so no mistake should be made in the darkness. The rest soon followed, and one beat in the door with a sledge hammer, whilst another stood in the street with a loaded horse-pistol, threatening to blow out the Exciseman's brains, or that of any other person who offered resistance. Having secured the goods they soon loaded their carts and horses,

Local ales are from the Hall & Wood-house brewery at Blandford.

and with an armed outrider in front and another as rear guard galloped away.

To me the most intriguing aspect of this story is in regard to Lewis Tregonwell, who for many years was revered as 'The Founder of Bournemouth' (see the Royal Exeter Hotel).

There is documentary evidence, mostly in private diaries, to confirm that members of the gentry colluded in funding and organising smuggling activities and it appears that Tregon-well could well have been among them.

Born in Anderson, Dorset in 1758, Tregonwell later lived here at Cranborne Lodge, opposite the pub, and as we have already discovered had a servant cum butler called Thomas Symes (sometimes spelt Syms or Sims) who was a member of the local family of smugglers.

The Symes clan of Cranborne, Verwood and Sixpenny Hand-ley had long been involved in smuggling.

The Exciseman's house stood at the corner of the street opposite the pub.

Today the seventeenth-century Inn at Cranborne is a particularly civilised place. There is one long main bar/dining room with a number of cosy corners. Decoration and furnishings are traditional with wood-burning stoves in the feature fireplaces. The true antiquity of the building is very apparent in the smaller heavily-beamed bar room at the far end.

The menu is imaginative and it is easy to believe the claim that ingredients are locally sourced wherever possible. This prodigious Hall & Woodhouse pub still functions as an inn with en suite bathrooms provided in each of the four double rooms.

Lewis Tregonwell, revered as 'The Founder of Bournemouth' lived here at Cranborne Lodge across from the pub.

The Kings Arms in Whitecliffe Mill Street stands on the site where the Great Fire of Blandford started in 1731.

Blandford Forum [Map 3G]

The Kings Arms Hotel

Whitecliffe Mill Street, DT11 7BE Tel: 01258 452163

BLANDFORD CIVIC SOCIETY
THE KINGS ARMS
Built on the site of a tallow chandler's where the Great Fire of 1731 started.

Blandford Forum is situated between Cranborne Chase and the Dorset Downs, in the south-eastern corner of the Blackmore Vale. It is 15 miles northwest of Poole and 22 miles southwest of Salisbury.

Blandford is often cited as an example of a unique Georgian town because the centre was rebuilt in the eighteenth century, following the Great Fire of 1731. The fire started at 2 pm on 4 June

Patrons of the pub watched from these windows as Gulliver's posse passed by on a March evening in 1788.

in a tallow chandlers shop which occupied the site where the Kings Arms now stands.

A bricked-up tunnel entrance in the cellar of the Kings Arms.

The town also has historic military connections. In 1724 a troop of Hussars was stationed at Blandford who could be called on to assist Revenue officers in their anti-smuggling duties.

The main inland routes for smuggled goods landed at Bournemouth and Poole were through Blandford and then on to Bristol or Salisbury. Contraband was also transported up the River Stour from Christchurch. The town became a freight depot with contraband hidden in and under buildings and in pits on Bryanston common waiting for the time it could be safely moved onward.

In the late 1700s Isaac Gulliver and his family were in residence at the former

The former bonded store and house of the Blandford Supervisor of Customs in Whitcliffe Mill Street now functions as a care home.

Blacksmith's Arms, at Thorney Down on the main road from Blandford to Salisbury. On a cold spring morning in March 1788 Excise men found and seized nine casks of liquor and more than three quarters of a ton of tea at nearby Tidpit Down where Gulliver's gang regularly sold their contraband at an open market.

The original doors of the warehouse, which were subject to Gulliver's attack, are now displayed against the flank wall of the Blandford Museum in Bere's Yard off the market place.

The 'philistines' carried off the goods back to Blandford and locked them in the bonded warehouse in Whitecliffe Mill Street. The contraband would eventually have been taken all the way back to Poole to be sold by auction at the Custom House but things took an unexpected turn.

It did not take long for the news of the seizure to reach Gulliver and by the afternoon he had assembled a mounted posse of a hundred and fifty men. His aim was to reach Blandford by sundown, break into the warehouse and retrieve his goods. He instructed his blacksmith to stash some large crowbars in a cart together with chains which would be attached to the horse's traces to wrench the warehouse doors off their hinges.

As evening approached the armed cavalcade entered the town making their way down Salisbury Street to the five-way junction by the Kings Arms. They had to turn back almost at right angles to proceed up Whitecliffe Mill Street and the noise drew drinkers from the pub to see what was happening. Some of the regulars would have already seen the Revenue men bring their bounty into the town earlier in the day.

The bonded store was attached to the house of the Blandford Supervisor of Customs. By the time Gulliver's men had burst open the doors a large crowd of cheering onlookers had assembled. The jubilant smugglers made their way back down to the junction with what they regarded as their own property. As they carried it off through the town, firing their pistols into the air, they passed a couple of the retrieved casks to the good townsfolk. The delighted crowd acted more like they were witnessing a circus rather than an audacious crime. The historic old pub which occupies a prominent location in the town is currently the subject of a proposed refurbishment. At this time there are four bars and a courtyard at the rear. There are also five letting rooms and a breakfast room on the first floor and a sixth letting room on the ground floor.

The River Stour, seen from the big bridge in Blandford, was a contraband route for goods landed at Christchurch.

Okeford Fitzpaine [Map 3F]

The Royal Oak

Lower Street, Okeford Fitzpaine DT11 0RN Tel: 01258 861561

Set in the heart of the Dorset Downs in the north of the county, Okeford Fitzpaine is surrounded by beautiful countryside and typifies the best of English community life. The parish encompasses the neighbouring village of Fiddleford and the hamlet of Belchalwell.

In 1774 a lengthy enquiry into the state of smuggling in the area concluded: 'Issac Gulliver, William Beale and Roger Ridout run great quantities of goods from our North Shore between Poole and Christchurch.'

The Royal Oak today is a very popular two bar free house.

The village bar where Ridout's descendants still enjoy a drink by the big inglenook fireplace.

It seems that Roger Ridout, who worked with Isaac Gulliver, was involved with the overland transportation of contraband. The Ridout gang, who achieved legendary status in north Dorset, used to leave the occasional nocturnal bribe of a keg of brandy on the doorstep of Thomas Dashwood, the local magistrate who lived at Vine House in Sturminster Newton's Penny Street.

Writing in 1895, H. C. Dashwood, the JP's grandson gave an account of the smuggling era: 'My father stated that when a boy, in or about 1794, he had, when riding late at night seen the string of horses in the narrow road between Okeford Fitz-paine and Fiddleford with the kegs and other contraband goods on the horses. One or two men, armed, generally were in front and then ten or twelve horses connected by ropes or halters followed at a hard trot, and two or three men brought up the rear.'

The Royal Oak is a free house offering a changing selection of West Country ales.

'This cavalcade did not stop for any person, and it was very difficult to get out of their way, as the roads, until the turnpikes were made, would only allow for one carriage, except in certain places. The contraband goods were principally brought from Lulworth and the coast through Whiteparish and Okeford Fitzpaine, through the paths in the woods to Fiddleford, and thus distributed.'

Roger Ridout was born at Shroton near Blandford in 1736 and was only ten when he inherited a dwelling house and orchard near Fiddleford. He married at twenty and moved to Fiddleford where he augmented his income as a miller with proceeds from smuggling. Sometime between 1746 and 1784 he moved again to 'the Mills' on the Okeford Fitzpaine to Shillingstone road.

Good pub grub is served in the larger dining room bar.

Ridout's main storage facility was at Fiddleford Mill and Farm where the tenants kept the barton and stalls well stocked with hay and straw for concealing contraband.

Unlike his associate Isaac Gulliver,

Okeford Fitzpaine today is a peaceful picture postcard village.

Roger Ridout was not as successful in evading the law. In 1787 he was sent to Dorchester Jail for smuggling but managed to raise the £40 fine and was released within a fortnight. Presumably he had been apprehended outside of his home territory and Dashwood's jurisdiction.

The gravestone of Roger and Mary Ridout in the churchyard at Okeford Fitzpaine. Mary died in 1809 and Roger two years later.

Family folklore tells how when languishing in jail Roger was fortified by his wife Mary who would walk the 40-mile round trip from Okeford with a concealed bladder of brandy in her bosom. The container had a tube attached which she would pass through the bars so her husband could enjoy a sly tipple.

Roger and Mary had seven sons and their descendants still live in the village today. Okeford Fitzpaine's involvement in smuggling continued well into the nineteenth century by which time a Ridout was landlord of the Royal Oak. 'Ducky' Pope took over leadership of the gang and the 1825 Dorchester jail records included the name of Joseph Ridout, a grandson of Roger and Mary.

The Royal Oak is the only pub left of the various licensed and unlicensed premises that catered to the thirst of the villagers through the centuries. Today this is a very welcoming and popular two bar free house with an additional small dining room at the rear.

The pub has a car park and beer garden and hosts a well attended annual beer festival. Good pub grub is available every day plus a choice of roasts on Sunday.

ISLE OF PURBECK

Studland [Map 6H]

Bankes Arms

Manor Road, Studland BH19 3AU   Tel: 01929 450225

www.bankesarms.com/index.php

Studland is a village on the Isle of Purbeck located about two miles north of the town of Swanage, over a steep chalk ridge. Studland Bay is protected from the prevailing south-westerly winds and storms by Ballard Down and Handfast Point, the chalk headland which separates Studland from Swanage Bay to the south.

The Bankes Arms today. The stables were later incorporated into the main building as the Horseshoe Bar.

Above left: The Bankes Arms has a larger selection of real ales than any other Purbeck pub.

Above right: The Horseshoe Bar was formerly the stables to the inn.

In the seventeenth century a process of sand accumulation in the bay and along the South Haven Peninsula stretching north resulted in natural land reclamation and the creation or expansion of the bay's beaches and sand dune system.

The Smuggling History

Today the area around Studland is a haven for nature lovers and outdoor enthusiasts. During the seventeenth and eighteenth centuries it became a smugglers' paradise. The smooth sandy bed of the bay and the gentle slope of the beach made for easier landings on moonless nights. The tubs of spirits could then be easily hidden under sand, bracken or piles of seaweed.

Little Beach (now renamed by the National Trust 'South Beach') was one of the principal landing places for smuggled goods on the south coast. Behind the beach deep-cut lanes and gorges, often shrouded in foliage, led inland across the heath.

As far back as 1682 Treasury Investigator William Cullingford reported that smuggling vessels were anchoring almost daily in Studland Bay, landing some of their goods on Studland beach and transporting the rest in 'dragger boats' to Brownsea Island and later to Poole itself.

The garden, across the road from the pub, has sea and cliff views and masses of seating.

A century later there was a bitter dispute between another Customs boatman Thomas Hutchins and a smuggler called John Sinick. In 1786 Hutchins seized three casks of spirits from Sinick who later attempted to break into Hutchin's house to retrieve them. At his trial Sinick countered by accusing Hutchins of buying smuggled tea.

Things came to a head a few days later on Studland beach when Sinick and his wife were involved in unloading tubs of brandy from a canoe. The Customs man tried to seize a cask and a fight ensued in which Hutchins would have certainly been drowned but for the intervention of a passer-by.

In the foreground is the cottage used as the Wellington Arms and in the background is the New Inn, now named the Bankes Arms.

In 1827, two years after the coastguard cottages were built at Studland, local farmer George Damon became the landlord of the New Inn. It was the last remaining alehouse at Studland and was situated on the other side of the road from today's pub, on land owned by the wealthy Bankes family.

Like many other publicans at that time, being landlord was only a part time job for Damon who also owned and farmed thirty two acres of land in the heart of the village. On his death in 1844 William Lawrence took over the tenancy at £8 per annum. Lawrence renamed the New Inn the Wellington Arms in honour of the Duke of Wellington with whom he had fought in the Peninsular War right up to Waterloo. Many returning soldiers set up public houses with their severance pay on leaving the army.

At this time virtually every inhabitant of Studland was involved in smuggling. Lawrence did not fare too well initially as a landlord and after a short while he got into debt. However, these debts were paid off by the end of 1846 and after that business thrived. It seems most likely that Lawrence's change of fortune was due to his involvement with the local smuggling trade.

Studland beach looking across the bay to Handfast Point with old Harry Rocks in the centre background.

From the beach, smugglers' trails led off across the dunes.

Lawrence retired in 1856 and the Wellington Arms was taken over by Moses Gould, who farmed Kingswood Farm and renamed the pub The New Inn. William Lawrence's autobiography *A Dorset Soldier* gives a detailed view into his life during and after his service.

In the late nineteenth century the quaint old thatched New Inn was rebuilt and renamed the Bankes Arms after the local landowning family.

The comfortably basic, friendly and easy-going big bar has a raised drinking area. There are beams, flagstones and two log fires. In addition there are ten good-sized bedrooms mostly en suite, many with sea views.

Over the years a stable bar to the rear was brought into use. The Lightdown family have owned the Bankes Arms since 1988 and have added a very successful micro-brewery producing the pub's own Isle of Purbeck ale. The pub is the perfect setting for eating al fresco while enjoying sea and cliff views from a huge garden with masses of seating across the road.

Above the sanctuary of the thirteenth-century St Nicholas church (seen on the far left) there is a room that can only be reached through a small door 20 feet up on the north side. During the eighteenth century this chamber was used to store contraband and legend has it that illicit goods were moved in and out during services.

The eighteenth-century King's Arms fronts the straggling village street of Langton Matravers.

Langton Matravers [Map 6H]

The King's Arms

27 High Street, Langton Matravers BH19 3HA Tel: 01929 422979

The straggling village of Langton Matravers, a couple of miles inland from Swanage, stretches for a considerable distance along a steadily rising road leading to Purbeck coastal hills. It was once largely occupied by workers from the nearby stone quarries. Like the farm labourers of agricultural Dorset and the fishermen of other coastal villages many quarrymen welcomed the opportunity to supplement their incomes with a little smuggling.

Steep cliffs in this area restricted the number of suitable places for landing goods but this was compensated for by the honeycomb of stone workings which provided a wealth of opportunities for concealing contraband.

Above left: Generations of quarrymen smugglers slaked the dust from their throats in the bar of the King's Arms.

Above right: Doors off the central passage give access to a series of cottagey rooms.

The men knew all the roads and paths, rocks and footholds, and could run about the cliffs as easily and safely as goats, whereas the coastguards, patrolling the cliffs at night, kept to their narrow track along the edge, clearly defined by a dotted line of white-washed stones.

Between Durlston and St Alban's Head, the only possibilities for landings were at Seacombe, Winspit and Dancing Ledge. The most remarkable smuggler from Langton Matravers was Charles Hayward, sexton and churchwarden of St George's church who rented Dancing Ledge quarry a mile to the south of the village.

The King's Arms is further down the hill on the opposite side of the road from the church. Hayward and his smuggling colleagues used to meet in a private room here to discuss strategy. The landlord was naturally sympathetic to the cause. Charlie Dean, Hayward's grandson recorded an event in his

The contraband was transported from the quarry in a horse-drawn wagon under a ton or two of stone.

diary which occurred on 23 October 1869. His grandfather had asked him to stand watch outside the church:

'Seven gentlemen arrived variously to meet my grandfather, and they all went inside the church. A Peeler [policeman] came down the road from Garfield, past me, and thence on to Stepps [Steppes]. I had given the alert (taking my cap off, shaking it, and putting it on again) and whilst the Peeler walked by all was silent in the church, nor any light. Presently came two stone-carts from Garfield end, and the seven gentlemen came out and assisted the drivers with unloading the stones; these were stacked flat-down and not up-down. The men then brought in barrels of all sizes and different shapes. All together this went into the church – I could not see where.'

Charles Hayward, smuggling church warden, whose memorial in St George's parish church states that he was: 'thirty three years clerk to this Parish'.

When inside the church the tubs were stored in a void above the ceiling which eventually took its toll on the fabric of the building. In 1874, Rev'd Trotman observed that the church was in a 'deplorable condition' and that 'The wide-spanning roof is pushing the walls out of the perpendicular.' The body of the church, excluding the tower, finally had to be demolished and re-built, opening again in 1876.

This pleasing architectural jigsaw puzzle of a pub was created from adjoining cottages and farm buildings over at least three hundred years. Although the main part of the building dates from the late eighteenth century the back or south section dates from around 1740.

Originally called the Mason's Arms, the pub had a series of landlords associated with the stone trade before Strong & Company of Romsey purchased it in 1882. William Marshfield, who was landlord during the time of the Napoleonic era, patriotically changed the name to the King's Arms.

Marks in the wall of St George's church show the position of the original roofline.

The honeycomb of quarries and man-made caves provided a wealth of opportunities for concealing contraband.

He once avoided serving time in Dorchester jail because embarrassed customs men failed to search the premises thoroughly. Marshfield's wife was crying in agony with labour pains in an upstairs room where contraband was concealed under the bed. In later life, as an old lady, the Marshfield's daughter would tell how she came to be born on top of two barrels of smuggled brandy.

The King's Arms was purchased from the brewery in 1993 and has remained a free house from that time. This quirky friendly place serves well kept ale and wholesome food but I doubt the word 'gastro' has ever been uttered within its ancient walls.

Throughout the smuggling period vast quantities of contraband were hidden in these man-made caverns.

The Square & Compass began life as a pair of cottages commanding a little bluff over-looking the village and with a marvellous view of the Channel.

Worth Matravers [Map 6H]
The Square & Compass

Swanage, Dorset BH19 3LF Tel: 01929 439229

www.squareandcompasspub.co.uk

Worth Matravers is beautifully situated on the limestone cliffs west of Swanage. It stands at the head of a valley running down between lynchet-striated slopes to the popular bathing ledges of Winspit. Once thriving on the local stone, farming and fishing industries, Worth has retired into a weekend refuge.

The village of Worth Matravers was a control centre for many local smuggling operations. Today there is a 3 mile circular 'Smugglers' Ways Walk' which begins at Worth Matravers and leads to Winspit Quarry, along the South West Coast Path

The front door opens to a view of the sea.

to Seacombe. The trail was once used by Smugglers, who under the cover of darkness, would hide their contraband in the caves and tunnels along the way.

Above left: There is no bar counter at 'the Square' just this original simple serving hatch.

Above right: The interior of this wonderful quirky place comprises a couple of small character-filled rooms.

An 1804 report from Poole Custom House about the landing places near Worth Matravers says: 'At the first place neither carriages nor horses can approach the shore nearer than half-a-mile, in consequence of which small quantities only are landed and which are conveyed from the boats to the carriages by the smugglers themselves.'

Most of the smugglers were quarrymen, and therefore had business in these lurking places. There are tales of skirmishes

The small (free) museum exhibits local fossils and artefacts, mostly collected by the friendly current landlord and his father.

with Excisemen at St Alban's Head and one smuggler whose breast had been pierced by a musket ball was carried to the Square & Compass where he died of his wounds.

This unchanging country tavern, with masses of character, began life as a pair of cottages commanding a little bluff overlooking the village and with a marvellous view of the Channel. Around 1776, it became an alehouse, owned by a Wareham brewer, cum clay merchant, under the sign of The Sloop.

From the rustic garden benches you can enjoy fantastic views over the village rooftops and down to the sea while free-roaming chickens and other birds go clucking around your feet.

A new tenant landlord, a stone mason called Charles Bower, seems to have changed the name around 1830. He ran the place for more than forty years, to be followed by his widow and then a series of tenants until 1907.

In March 1907, Charlie and Florence Newman, newly married, took the tenancy from the brewers, Strong and Co, moving from Wareham's Red Lion to this rural backwater. The pub is now in the hands of the third generation of Newmans.

In 1994 the current Charlie Newman bought the pub from the brewer and in 1998 he opened a museum to house both his father's and his own collection of fossils and archaeological items.

The pub sign depicting the tools of the local stonemason's craft which are now recognised as the international symbols for Freemasonry.

Charlie moved to a back seat role in 2003 handing over to manager Kevin Hunt. In 2008 he married Cath Bradshaw and dedicated himself to cider manufacture and furthering his fossil collection. The 'Square' offers simple tasty snacks and Palmers Copper with guest ales from brewers such as Cottage, Frys and Otley plus up to ten ciders tapped from a row of casks.

Chapman's Pool smugglers' landing cove.

The Weld Arms is a seventeenth-century thatched pub and was originally a row of cottages built for estate workers by the Weld family whose descendants live in the nearby castle.

East Lulworth [Map 6G]

The Weld Arms

East Lulworth, Wareham BH20 5QQ Tel: 01929 400 211

East Lulworth is a pretty, well cared-for stone village consisting of old thatched cottages and its historic pub, the Weld Arms, named after the Lulworth Lords of the Manor.

The Lulworth Estate extends over 20 square miles of the south Dorset countryside, including 5 miles of the Jurassic Coast and the internationally-renowned landmarks of Lulworth Cove and Durdle Door.

The isolated beach at Arish Mell, due south of Lulworth Castle, was the site of numerous illicit landings and some violence. In April 1719, Weymouth Customs Officer Philip Taylor and his men made a search of all the property in East Lulworth including the Castle, home of Humphrey Weld whose descendants are still squires of Lulworth today.

Taylor found nothing in the Castle, but Edward Bagwell, a tenant of Mr Weld was caught with four gallons of brandy

There is a bar with bar stools but the emphasis here is firmly on dining.

Above left: Today's plush interior at the Weld Arms would be unrecognisable to smuggler Richard Champ who ran the pub in the late 1700s.
Above right: The attractive little snug dining room with wood burning stove.

and twelve pounds of pepper. At three o'clock in the morning of the following day a big battle ensued between the Customs men and smugglers which lasted for twelve hours. The officers managed to seize several casks of wine and brandy but the majority 'was carried off from the smugglers by the country people of three or four parishes'.

The leaders of the smugglers, William and Roger Keats and William Stanley made use of swords and flails. They were arrested and all convicted of assault at Dorset Assizes, despite separate petitions from three gentlemen pleading on Stanley's behalf. Their sentences were negligible and within a few weeks they were out and up to their old tricks.

The Weld Arms was run by Richard Champ around 1770 who operated with the well-known gang of smugglers from Osmington Mills run by Emmanuel Charles, landlord of the then Crown Inn. Members of the Charles family intermarried many times with the local smuggling Seaward and Champ families.

An 1804 report on smuggling at East Lulworth from the Weymouth Custom House stated: 'The places for landing smuggled goods to the eastward of this place are Jordan Gate, Upton Mills, Ringstead Beach, Mupe, Arish Mill [Mell] and Worbarrow Beach. The three latter are the most noted places.'

'It frequently happens that large vessels carrying from four to six or seven hundred casks land their cargoes at these places, which vessels do not belong to or are known to any in this part of the coast. This they carry off in defiance to the officers on the station and which ... we suppose may amount to ten thousand casks annually ...'

Worbarrow Bay, former smuggling landing beach at East Lulworth.

Lulworth Castle with its smuggling connections was purchased by Humphrey Weld in 1641 and is still lived in by his direct descendants.

Probably the greatest hideout and smugglers haunt along this coast was Lulworth Castle, the seat of the Weld family, which had a connection with smuggling throughout the eighteenth and nineteenth centuries. Maids working at the castle would routinely warn smugglers when the Customs men were in the vicinity by showing a light at a window to indicate when it was safe to proceed.

Lulworth Castle was built in the early seventeenth century as a lodge to entertain hunting parties for the King and Court. The Howards owned it until 1641 when it was purchased by Humphrey Weld, the direct ancestor of the present owners.

The exterior of the Castle has changed little over the years but the interior evolved in line with changing fashions until it was gutted by a disastrous fire in 1929. Restoration work continued until 1989 when the Castle opened its doors to the public as a tourist attraction.

The seventeenth-century thatched pub was originally a row of cottages built for estate workers by the Weld family. The Weld Arms today is friendly with a nice mix of individual furnishings. There is an attractive little snug and a civilised log-fire bar plus two dining rooms. Outside there are picnic-sets in the large rambling garden.

If you like dog-friendly pubs, the Castle Inn at West Lulworth will not disappoint.

West Lulworth [Map 6G]

The Castle Inn

The Castle Inn, Main Road, West Lulworth BH20 5RN   Tel: 01929 400311

www.thecastleinn-lulworthcove.co.uk

The village of West Lulworth is about half a mile due north of the famous sheltered bay of Lulworth Cove which has been described as the most beautiful in Britain, making an almost perfect circle, surrounded on all sides by hills and cliffs.

The Castle Inn still retains its picture postcard appearance.

Of all the contraband landing places on this part of the coast during the early eighteenth century, Lulworth was the most popular or, according to Philip Taylor, Collector of Customs at Weymouth, 'the most notorious'. This extremely sheltered bay could be used in virtually all weathers, and was of course the ideal spot to sink tubs.

A report in *The Western Flying*

Post in June 1777 said: 'Some days since a Dunkirk schooner landed near Arish Mell on the Dorchester coast upwards of twenty tons of tea, in sight of and in defiance of the Custom House officers and others, as they were mounted twenty-four pounders, which she brought to bear on the beach.'

There was a time when things were much more exciting around here.

'The smugglers on shore carried it off in three waggons and on horses, except twelve hundred weight which officers seized and carried to a public house at West Lulworth two miles from the place of landing; but thirty or forty of the schooner's people, well-armed, followed after and broke into the house beating and cutting the people they found there in a cruel manner.'

Philip Newton and John Gregory, the Riding Officer and Boatman at Lulworth were completely corrupt and in league with the smugglers. Not only did they accept bribes they even commissioned smugglers to bring them brandy over from France.

In the early years of the eighteenth century the local venturer at Lulworth was Charles Weeks, who developed a particularly shrewd way of defrauding the Revenue. He would buy seized goods at legitimate auctions, and mix in the smuggled article for onward shipment, often to London. When an officer challenged the smuggler to produce receipts showing that duty had been paid, Weeks could often do so.

Below left: The attractive bar counter is decorated with colourful sea shells collected at the cove.

Below right: Inside there is a maze of booth seating in the quaintly divided flagstoned bar.

The pub garden is located high at the back of the inn offering views across the Dorset hills.

The cove at Lulworth has been described as the most beautiful in Britain making an almost perfect circle surrounded on all sides by hills and cliffs.

The sixteenth-century Castle Inn in West Lulworth is within walking distance of Lulworth Cove. The pub has changed names many times during its history, being variously known as the Green Man, the Smugglers Inn and the Jolly Sailor but finally changed from this to its present name in 1929 when Lulworth Castle burned down.

There is a maze of booth seating in the quaintly divided flagstoned bar. Plus a more modern separate lounge bar and a pleasant restaurant. Today the Castle Inn acts as a popular traditional pub and hotel, owned by the Halliday family for over twenty-six years as a freehold. As well as great food, there is a focus upon traditional Real Ales, Real Ciders and Perries.

Some of the Lulworth coastguard cottages are lived in today by descendants of the original smugglers.

The Ship Inn at Wool is a large and homely pub-restaurant where meals are served all day.

Wool [Map 5G]

The Ship Inn

Wool, Wareham BH20 6EQ Tel: 01929 462247

www.shipwool.co.uk

The village of Wool lies at a historic bridging point on the River Frome, half way between Dorchester and Wareham. Much has changed since the heyday of smuggling (particularly because of the coming of the railway) but some sense of the history can still be appreciated with the thatched cottages along Spring Street.

Smuggling Chief Tom Lucas was landlord here in the 1820s when the pub occupied the right hand one of this former row of cottages.

The regular route that contraband followed inland from Lulworth went directly through the village of Wool. In 1779 a 'large and desperate' gang of smugglers clashed here with Revenue men and soldiers from Dorchester. At least one smuggler was shot dead and a newspaper reported that 'many more were wounded'. The seizure included 300 gallons of brandy and gin, 2,300 pounds of tea and 32 of the smugglers' horses.

In the 1820s the landlord of the Ship Inn was smuggler Tom Lucas. He was a formidable man who was involved in the landings of contraband and supervised storage and onward shipment of the goods. Lucas and his associates were notorious for their violence and their armoury included pistols, swords, bludgeons, poles and a particularly nasty flail-type weapon called a swingle which could be flung whiplash-style around someone's body with deadly effect.

Eventually, in 1827, after a clash near St Alban's Head which caused the death of two coastguards, several leaders of the Wool gang were identified. The authorities called for the assistance of Bow Street Runners from London to deal with them.

The spacious interior is divided into separate dining areas.

Above left: The pub is decorated with a collection of maritime artefacts and prints.

Above right: Today there is a warm welcome and a broad and inviting menu in this old Badger Inn.

The heavily-armed law enforcers arrived in large numbers in the early hours of the morning. Approaching quietly one of them knocked gently on the door. When Lucas asked 'Who's there?' the officer replied in a childlike voice 'It's only me, Mr Lucas, Mrs Smith's little girl. I want a little drop of brandy for mother, for she is bad in her bowels.'

The subterfuge worked, and when Lucas opened the door, he was arrested by several burly sergeants, and hustled off to Dorchester jail where he found himself reunited with five of his comrades. The charges against four of the six were later dropped. Lucas and one other were tried but acquitted, perhaps by a jury fearful of the consequences of a guilty verdict.

The jail records show that not all the smugglers from Wool escaped conviction. The list of names includes Edith Mead, aged sixty-three, and William Hurst, thirty-nine who served six and seven months respectively for smuggling in 1803. George Langdon a thirty-seven-year old labourer was caught conveying smuggled brandy in 1813, and twenty-five-year old Thomas Stickland, also a labourer, was sentenced to two months hard labour in 1825 for making a light on the coast as a signal to smugglers.

The front of the building is listed but the interior has been changed out of recognition since Tom Lucas was landlord here. There has also been a rear extension to the building which has doubled its size.

Refurbished in the summer of 2012 this smart pub restaurant has a comfortable traditional feel with beams and fireplaces and is decorated with maritime prints and artefacts.

Former smugglers' cottages standing back from the little stream in Spring Street present an attractive peaceful scene today.

CHESIL BEACH AND WEYMOUTH

Osmington Mills [Map 6F]

The Smugglers Inn

Osmington Mills, Weymouth DT3 6HF Tel: 01305 833125

smugglersinn.weymouth@hall-woodhouse.co.uk

The Smugglers Inn at Osmington Mills was originally known as The Crown, and later the Picnic Inn.

About halfway between West Lulworth and Weymouth there is a secluded valley hidden from casual gaze among the surrounding high cliffs. Sheltered in this idyllic location is the picturesque village of Osmington Mills with its historic pub and little stream running down to the sea.

Like many of Dorset's surviving smugglers pubs the Smugglers Inn has expanded from its small beginnings and now occupies a complete row of cottages.

An easy landing and a safe route inland made this a valuable location for import smugglers. The original thirteenth-century inn had a constant flow of visitors, both English and foreign, and a constant supply of smuggled liquor with which to supply them.

During the eighteenth and nineteenth centuries Osmington Mills was home to the Charles gang, one of the most notorious bands of smugglers in the area. In the 1820s Emmanuel Charles (sometimes spelt Carless), the leader of the gang, was landlord of the pub, which was known then as The Crown. The gang included a number of the landlord's ruthless family members who mercilessly set about preventive officers.

Emanuel Charles also provided shelter for the famous French smuggler Pierre Latour, known locally as French Peter. Latour, who used the pub as his headquarters, sailed a fast and lightly-armed cutter called *L'Hirondelle* (The Swallow). There is a local tale of French Peter arriving at the pub one day when newly appointed Revenue Officer John Tallman had hidden himself up the chimney hoping to hear the

Above left: This cosy corner by the wood burning stove is an ideal refuge on a winter's day.

Above right: The 'Smugg's Snug' was the original Crown Inn.

Frenchman's plans for contraband runs. When Latour entered the inn Emanuel offered him gin instead of his usual brandy and indicated with a nod towards the fireplace where the officer was hiding.

Latour caught on quickly and said: 'I'm feeling a bit of a sea-chill today Charles, perhaps I'll have a tot of brandy, and what about a warming fire in yonder grate.' The two men set to work with damp twigs, heather and rotting leaves, and soon the choking smoke brought the unfortunate Revenue man out of his hiding place. The hapless Tallman dusted himself off, sheepishly accepted a tot of brandy, and went on his way.

Apparently the brandy that Latour imported was 'so raw and unpalatable as to be totally unfit for consumption'. None of the locals would drink it and it had to be shipped inland disguised as luggage on the local mail coaches, then redistilled before it could be sold.

Latour, who earned a small fortune as a smuggler, eventually fell in love with the publican's daughter, Arabella. Their story did not have a happy ending. One night during a raid by local militia, Arabella was shot dead while trying to help her husband escape.

There has been an inn on the site of the current pub since the thirteenth century. Originally called The Crown, then the

Picnic before being aptly named the Smugglers Inn. Set on the cliffs at Osmington Mills with the South Coast Path running through the garden, the inn has beautiful views across Weymouth Bay to the Island of Portland.

This row of former coastguard cottages directly behind the pub is now private residences.

This partly thatched family-orientated inn has four bedrooms. The interior has been sympathetically extended, with cosy softly-lit timber divided areas, wood burners and old local pictures.

There are picnic sets on crazy paving by the little stream and a thatched summer bar, plus a play area. The parking charge is refunded at the bar when you use the pub.

The wonderful view from the pub car park and contraband landing beach across to the Island of Portland.

Today, the imposing Moon-fleet Manor Hotel is warm, welcoming and very family orientated.

Fleet [Map 6E]

Moonfleet Manor Hotel

Fleet Road, Weymouth DT3 4ED Tel: 01305 786948

www.visit-dorset.com/accommodation/moonfleet-manor-hotel

Fleet lies a couple of miles west of Weymouth behind the unique irregular seawater lagoon which separates most of Chesil Beach from the mainland. Here you will find the essential landmarks of the story of John Meade Falkner's *Moonfleet* and a pervading atmosphere of that bygone time.

Meade Falkner was brought up in Dorchester and Weymouth when the tradition of smuggling was still fresh in the minds of the fishing community. He used Fleet, its legends and setting for his 1898 novel which is one of the best adventure stories of the illicit free trade ever written.

Though fictional, the story had its foundations on the trade

that flourished here with its thriving commerce in spirits, tea, tobacco and lace. In 1717, Customs officials trying to prevent a landing on Chesil Beach reported that they were met by thirty men in disguise, who drove them away with clubs and other weapons.

Above left: The public rooms are furnished with beautiful genuine antiques.

Above right: The place is relaxed with no stuffy dress code.

Chesil Beach, and the Fleet Lagoon gave the smugglers from the Weymouth area a unique advantage. This extraordinary bank of shingle stretches unbroken nearly 17 miles, from Burton Bradstock to Portland.

Smugglers landing on the beach in the pitch black of a moonless night were able to judge their position to within a mile

The spacious restaurant has a timber decking terrace, both having views over the countryside and the Fleet Water.

Above left: Butter Street as it looked in John Meade Falkner's day.

Above right: 'Why Not Inn' cottage in Butter Street.

or two by simply picking up a handful of shingle, and gauging the average size of the stones. At the Portland end, the pebbles are the size of potatoes, and then progressively slim down to pea-shingle on the beach at Burton Bradstock. Tubs landed here were humped over Chesil Beach, and sunk in the quiet waters of the Fleet for collection at a more convenient time. Landing, however, was not always straightforward because in stormy weather a ferocious sea pounds Chesil Beach, often reducing vessels to matchwood. On one memorable occasion a 500 ton ship was swept clean over the beach and into the Fleet.

Though imposing, this family friendly hotel is warm and welcoming and there is no stuffy dress code. There is a spacious restaurant with a timber decking terrace, both overlooking the countryside and the Fleet Water.

Moonfleet (Mohune-Fleet) Manor Hotel is central to both John Meade Falkner's story and location. It stands on the edge of the Fleet Water at the end of the minor road. Many of the rooms in the hotel are named after characters in the book including Master Ratsey, Trenchard and Mohune.

The mansion was formerly called Fleet House, built by Maximillion Mohune in 1603, and extended and remodelled in 1806. Much of the Manor was rebuilt in 1889 – the year following Meade Falkner's story – but there are some remnants of the original Jacobean manor and the Georgian portico remains intact.

A footpath leads from the hotel to a group of cottages at Butter Street, one of which is named after the 'Why Not Inn'; the pub run by Elzevir Block, which plays such a prominent part in the story.

One of the most memorable heart-stopping episodes in the adventure takes place in the Mohune vault beneath the old church where the free traders hide their contraband and spread rumours of Blackbeard's ghost haunting the place to keep the inquisitive away.

This tiny chancel is all that remains of the old church which was inundated in the great storm of 1824, when the nave was wrecked. It was here that tubs bumped together in the flooded vault.

There is a date above the left ground floor window which reads 1621, but the rear of the building is known to be much older and opens directly opposite the beach.

Weymouth [6E]
The Black Dog

3 Saint Mary Street, Weymouth DT4 8PB Tel: 01305 771426

The resort of Weymouth is centrally situated along the Dorset coast. In 1789, King George III made his first visit to the town, recovering from a bout of porphyria. With its soft, golden sands and sheltered bay it became his favourite place. Following his lead, other visitors came and over two hundred years it has become a much loved summer holiday destination.

Throughout the smuggling era Weymouth was the centre of preventive operations for a wide area. However, Custom House correspondence suggests the preventive officers were not very effective. At the end of the seventeenth century, the Collector of Customs at Weymouth was described in a scathing official report which said he had: 'a debauched life and conversation, seldom sober, and hardly ever goes to bed till three or four a clock in the morning and many times not all night.' At one stage even the Mayor of Weymouth was a known smuggler who literally kept his officers sweet, with bribes of sugar and sherry.

This Elizabethan window frame is an internal feature of the pub. In 1758, in the room beyond, smuggler Richard Hawkins was whipped to death.

In the late 1730s, tea overtook brandy as the main contraband cargo. The smugglers themselves preferred alcoholic beverages and usually had their favourite inns and ale houses in the villages and towns. In 1739, the Board of Customs decided to get at the smugglers through the landlords and inn keepers. The owners of licenced hostelries were required by law to apply for renewal of their licences each year. The plan being to oppose certain applications for pubs that were known smugglers haunts. After initial enquires the Weymouth Customs

Above left: Dark beams and bare floorboards are a feature in the main bar area.
Above right: Founded in 1996, the Weymouth-based Dorset Brewing Company produces a special bitter for The Black Dog.

In February 1645, John Chiles and his wife Margaret robbed and murdered William Courtney who was staying in the pub. They carried the corpse along this back entry and dumped it in the sea.

Collector reported:

> *'Twill be a matter of great difficulty (if not impossible for us) to prove the country fellows that daily use our markets and public houses for buying of lobsters, crabs, oysters and all sorts of fish to be smugglers and known to be such by the occupiers of the several public houses in this town and parts adjacent'.*

The Black Dog in central Weymouth is reputed to be the oldest pub in town. In February 1645, during the English Civil War, five hundred people died in one bloody night during the Battle of Weymouth. At that time John Chiles and his wife Margaret were running the Black Dog which was then known as a 'house of entertainment'.

William Courtney, from Somerset, was lodging at the pub. He was described as a 'trader with flaxen hair and a yellow beard', who hailed from Taunton Deane. John and Margaret Chiles murdered him while he slept. They hit him on the head with a hammer in order to steal the £288 in gold and £12 in silver which he had with him.

The couple then stripped the body and, in the darkness, carried it through the back entry of the pub to a nearby jetty. They threw it into the sea, no doubt thinking that one more cadaver in a war zone would cause no particular suspicion. However, the body was recognised and the pair arrested. Margaret Chiles soon broke under questioning and gave evidence against her husband for the murder.

Built sometime during the reign of Elizabeth I, the pub was formerly known as 'The Dove' until Weymouth won the contract to trade with the new colonies of Newfoundland and Labrador.

The landlord (at the time) purchased the first black 'Newfoundland Labrador' from one of the new trading ships from that region. The dog was the first of its breed to be seen

Weymouth Custom House on the Quay was the centre of preventive operations for a wide area but reports suggest the officers were not very effective.

in the South West and apparently attracted an amazing number of sightseers. The landlord was so pleased he changed the name of the pub in honour of the dog which had brought him so much prosperity.

In 1758, when The Black Dog was a haunt for smugglers, one of them was murdered inside the pub. The foul deed, which resulted from an argument, occurred in front of the fireplace in the bar. John 'Smoaker' Mills the son of a local, Richard Mills, whipped Richard Hawkins to death.

The murder took place because Mills, an ally of the famous Hawkhurst smuggling gang of Kent, falsely accused Richard Hawkins of an offence against the gang. It was only later that it was found that Hawkins was entirely innocent of the accusations against him. The murderers were caught and later hanged at East Grinstead in West Sussex.

The eighteenth-century Cove House Inn is built into the sea defences.

Chiswell Village, Isle of Portland [Map 7E]

The Cove House Inn

91 Chiswell, Portland, Dorset DT5 1AW Tel: 01305 820895

Portland, off shore from Weymouth, is not really an island but is reached over a narrow causeway from Chesil Beach. It is a huge block of limestone, measuring 4½ by 1¾ miles rising to a height of nearly 500 feet above sea level in the north.

Chiswell is a fishing village at the southern end of Chesil Beach. The small bay is called Chesil Cove, and the village is built around it. Chiswell is the oldest settlement on the island and the promenade and sea wall, which form its coastal defences, are a prominent feature.

The three room interior was modified during the twentieth-century and features substantial dressed stone walls and bare board floors.

Below left: The long open windows looking straight out to sea are shuttered in the winter storms for protection.

Below right: The Cove House Inn is a free house with a varying choice of three real ales. They serve reasonably priced 'pubby' food (all day at weekends).

In his novel *The Well Beloved,* Thomas Hardy calls Portland 'The Isle of Slingers' because the inhospitable Portlanders used to throw stones to keep away strangers including Customs men.

A report of 1746 declared that the inhabitants of the island had become so 'audacious and insolent' that Customs men were reluctant to set foot on the island 'for fear of being knocked on the head by a volley of stones'.

Landing at night on Chesil Beach fishermen and smugglers

Chesil Beach and Portland seen from the pub during a moment of calm.

could tell where they were by the size of the pebbles which are duck egg size at Portland grading to pea shingle 18 miles further east.

In past storms, the sea has thrown pebbles onto the roof of the pub.

In 1747 the crew of the Revenue sloop *Cholmondeley* were stoned as they tried to search boats in the landwash near Portland Castle. The attack was launched by a mob of more than twenty strong, among whom were fishermen Robert Shaddick and John Ayles the elder, better known as 'Cat' Ayles, quarrymen Edward Toby, William Way and Alexander Attwool. Others of the slingers named were masons Edward Harris and John Ayles, commonly known as 'Merchant' Ayles. They were all residents of Chiswell and would have been patrons of the Cove House Inn.

The Dorchester jail records of Portland smugglers convicted between 1820 and 1840 included the names of more Portland residents than any other area of the county. The legitimate professions of these people include seamen, fishermen, fish-

Above left: At night, fishermen and smugglers could tell where they had landed on the beach by the size of the pebbles. Duck egg size pebbles at the Portland end of Chesil Beach...

Above right: ... grading to pea shingle 18 miles further east.

erwomen, fish carriers, washer women, needle women, stone masons, quarry men, carpenters, blacksmiths, grocers, bakers, shirt makers and cordwainers (shoemakers).

The low-beamed eighteenth-century Cove House Inn has been Grade II listed since May 1993. It is situated within the village of Chiswell, and lies next to Chesil Beach on the esplanade. Famed for its panoramic views, Cove House is one of Portland's most popular pubs.

Despite its particularly close proximity to the beach the pub survived the ferocious storm known as 'The Great Gale of 1824'. This storm destroyed a considerable amount of the surrounding Chiswell village.

The three-room interior was modified during the twentieth century and features substantial dressed stone walls. Settles and country style furniture stand on bare board flooring. The long open windows looking straight out to sea are shuttered in the winter storms for protection.

The Cove House Inn is a free house with a varying choice of three real ales and serves reasonably priced pubby food (all day at weekends). The Madeleine Tristan Bar is named after the French Schooner that was beached at Chesil during a September storm in 1930. Around the walls of this room are photographs of ships that have come to grief along this stretch of coast over the years.

Fronting the pub is an outside seating area overlooking the beach and the rugged cliffs of Portland peninsula.

The Elm Tree at Langton Herring is much extended from the fisherman's pub that the smugglers knew.

Langton Herring [Map 6E]
The Elm Tree Inn

Shop Lane, Langton Herring, Weymouth, Dorset DT3 4HU Tel: 01305 871257

www.theelmtreeinn.com

The little backwater village of Langton Herring is set on a ridge above the Fleet Lagoon about 5 miles northwest of Weymouth approximately halfway along the famous Chesil Beach. In common with the other villages along this coast, the inhabitants of Langton Herring were chiefly employed in fishing, agriculture and smuggling.

In 1746 the Langton Riding Officer Edward Bayley was obstructed while attempting to do his duty and the home of his colleague John Moise was broken into by smugglers who recovered 134 pounds of seized tea.

The original pub was simply a couple of rooms in this small cottage which forms part of the present day inn.

Dorchester jail records show that the Vivian family of Langton were particularly well known for smuggling. Five were convicted between 1818 and 1832, including fourteen-year-old Martha Vivian. Seventeen-year-old

This aerial photograph shows the proximity of St Peter's church which was said to be linked to the pub by a tunnel. Generations of smuggling fishermen lie in the churchyard.

fisherman John Vivian was sentenced in 1818 to three months hard labour for 'making a light and fire signal to person or persons on board a smuggling vessel'.

In addition to the Bartletts, Haggards and Carters, another Langton Herring family deeply involved in the free trade were the Wittles. One of them, William, a twenty-three-year-

For centuries Langton Herring fishermen have sat by this fire swapping tales of terrible storms, shipwrecks and smuggling.

gstone floors,
ginal beams
d built-in settles
: still part of the
bar.

Above left:
A cheating fisherman was hanged from this ship's mast beam in the old bar.

Above right: On the wall by the fireside is information about Ethel Gee who used to sit on the settle below with her spy lover Harry Houghton in the 1960s.

old seaman was sentenced to death in 1834 for: 'smuggling, assaulting preventative officers and feloniously assembling to the number of three or more to assist in landing and running prohibited goods.'

Wittle was later reprieved and his sentence commuted to transportation to Australia. Fellow convicts among the passengers were six Dorset agricultural labourers, famously known as the 'Tolpuddle Martyrs'.

In 1830 the weekly wage of a farm labourer was nine shillings, the following year it was reduced to eight shillings, and then to seven. In March 1834 the six men from Tolpuddle (20 miles north east of Langton Herring) met to discuss their desperate situation. They were arrested for unlawful assembly and charged with 'administering unlawful oaths'.

There was once a number of elms growing in and around the village and the pub takes its name from one large tree that stood nearby. The building is said to be about four hundred years old with some of the beams made from ships' timbers. One beam in the bar's ceiling was made from a mast and retains the hook on which a fisherman was hanged. The murder victim had deceived and cheated his fellow fishermen over the size of his catch and was ruthlessly chased through the village and subsequently hanged.

A paved area in the floor of the pub kitchen is thought to conceal either a contraband hiding place or the entrance to a tunnel leading to the adjacent church.

Today the pub has been greatly extended to incorporate a couple of large dining rooms.

Real ale is still dispensed straight from the cask as was always the custom in this historic pub.

More recently, in the 1960s, the bar of the Elm Tree became the focus of world interest. A couple who worked at Portland Naval Base were selling classified information to the Russians. It was in the bar that Harry Houghton and his mistress Ethel Gee met for a drink. They would sit beside the inglenook on the high-backed settle, before leaving secret messages for their Soviet masters in prearranged hiding places around the village.

Today the Elm Tree is a spacious dining pub with an emphasis on fish dishes. In addition to the traditional bar there are two large dining rooms. Outside is a pretty sunken garden with palm trees, flowering shrubs and tables for summer use.

Half a mile from the village, at the end of a stony track, are a row of coastguard cottages. They stand on the edge of the Fleet Lagoon whose passive waters were ideal for sinking tubs.

LYME BAY

Askerswell [Map 5D]

The Spyway Inn

The Spyway Inn, Askerswell, Dorset DT2 9EP Tel: 01308 485250

www.spyway-inn.co.uk

The small village of Askerswell, 5½ miles north-east of Abbotsbury, lies at the foot of the Iron Age Hillfort of Eggardon Camp. There are several ramparts and ditches still evident at the camp and it is an excellent viewpoint south to Golden Cap and the sea. Spyway is a small hamlet just north of Askerwell, accessed from the village via School Lane.

This family-run country inn fronts on to Spyway Hill.

The fun figure on the inn sign looks far more like a pirate than a smuggler.

Spyway Hill commemorates the area's contraband associations. At some time in the 1780s Isaac Gulliver purchased land here which included Eggardon Hill standing 252 metres above sea level, and North Eggardon Farm located below it. He planted pine trees on the summit of the hill as a sea-mark for his smuggling luggers.

He used outbuildings on the farm and caves in the hill to store contraband. Neighbouring farmers also provided storage even clearing away ancient bones to make funeral barrows available. Generations of contraband carriers passed this way along the old Roman Road, conveying their cargoes of spirits, wine, tea and tobacco to Yeovil, Bath and Bristol.

Gulliver's 'kingdom' eventually stretched the entire length of the Dorset coast. When establishing this western connection, he used the beaches of Burton Bradstock to unload his contra-

Eggardon Hill and farm, owned in the smuggling days by Issac Gulliver.

band. John Fryer, Gulliver's Poole associate, cheekily named one of his luggers *Eggardon Castle* after the hillfort. At the time, another pub called the Blue Boar stood on the other side of the valley near the present A35. The landlords of the Spyway Inn and the Blue Boar used to signal each other with lanterns when the way was clear to move the illicit goods.

Above left: The comfortable little snug bar to the left of the entrance.

Above right: The first of the two dining rooms with its wood burning stove.

This interesting old smuggler's inn dates back to 1745. It was first licensed a century later as the Three Horseshoes. Until 1905 the pub was attached to the village smithy and not renamed the Spyway until 1974.

The unspoilt little rooms at this simple, family-run country inn are cosily filled with old-fashioned high-backed settles, cushioned wall and window seats and some tub chairs. Old photos of the pub and rustic scenes decorate the walls and jugs hang from the beams.

The main dining room has oak beams and uprights, red cushioned dining chairs and dark tables on patterned carpet. Horse tack and horse brasses make reference to its former uses as a smithy and leading off are two smaller dining rooms.

The Spyway Inn is a free house serving West Country ales and generous helpings of really good food. Accommodation is also available in delightfully furnished, light and elegant rooms.

Left: This attractive little bar is for serving customers in the snug.

Right: Built on a hill, the pub interior has an interesting 'up along-down along' feel.

Situated in beautiful countryside, the rear beer garden and the back terrace provide magnificent views of the downs towards the coast. There is a large parking area and the pub is open seven days a week.

Askerswell church tower forms part of the view from the pub garden.

Seatown nestles below the imposing cliff of Golden Cap, the highest point in Dorset at 618 feet. A row of black coastguard cottages can be seen behind the pub.

Seatown [5C]

The Anchor Inn

www.theanchorinnseatown.co.uk Tel: 01297 489215

Seatown nestles just below the imposing cliff of Golden Cap, the highest point in Dorset at 618 feet. To reach the hamlet, turn south into Duck Street opposite Chideock church and follow the signs to the sea. It is approximately three quarters of a mile down a narrow winding lane with few passing places.

Prior to the great storm of 1824 Seatown was a much larger place. A farm and cottages that once stood beyond the Anchor Inn were swept away in the deluge.

From notes made by two local clergymen, Curate T. Worthington and later Reverend C. V. Goddard it is clear that nearly

Above left: The Anchor has two small bars which get very busy in summer.

Above right: Log burners in both rooms make this a snug shelter in winter.

everybody in Chideock and Seatown was involved to a greater or lesser extent in the free trade.

Worthington wrote: 'There used to be 30 to 40 fishermen at Seatown, ostensibly employed in their lawful avocations, but really smuggling.' The foremost smuggling families of Bartletts, Farewells, Oxenburys and Orchards led the way. Sam Bartlett, who had been brought up in the smuggling trade, was Reverend Goddard's churchwarden at Chideock. Goddard left us this observation:

The walls are decorated with maritime memorabilia and lots of interesting local photographs.

'The fishing interest seems to have slipped away with the dwellings at Seatown. Some say the fish have left the coast but others (with whom I agree) that in the old days the fishermen lived more by smuggling than fishing. They were a hardy lot, and the son of one of them, himself engaged in the trade as a youth, recalls the smuggling yarns that he, as a little boy, used to hear them tell and the adventures in which he later took part.'

'There were wild rushes to the West Rocks (beneath Golden Cap) when a boatload of spirits was being rowed ashore from a ship lying out to sea, each man readily shouldering his share of the load – two small kegs – and scrambling off as fast as his legs would carry him. He would find his own way inland to a safe retreat.'

At one time the Chideock smugglers, led by a man simply known as 'the Colonel', landed goods between Charmouth and Seatown, and marked the hills above their favoured landfalls (as Gulliver marked Eggardon Hill) with copses of trees.

There is a good selection of Palmers Ales and the menu suits all tastes from the walker seeking refuelling to the serious gourmet looking to enjoying a bowl of super fresh shellfish.

This unique nineteenth-century photograph shows coastguards checking two recently landed boats.

These grew at Charmouth, Seatown, Eype's Mouth and the lonely Stanton St Gabriel.

Riding Officers, attempting to gather information on local smuggling activities were hopelessly outnumbered. It was common for them to meet their end at the hands of the smugglers, pushed off the cliffs, drowned or bludgeoned to death. It is said one was murdered in an upper room at the Anchor Inn.

In 1820 the admiralty built a Watch House here and in 1840 five four-roomed coastguard cottages which still stand behind the pub today.

Quiet corners can be found in the pub out of season.

This strikingly situated Anchor Inn enjoys a unique location standing almost on the beach in a little cove surrounded by National Trust land and very near the Dorset Coast Path. The pub nestles dramatically in the lee of the Golden Cap pinnacle.

The large sun terrace and cliff-side beer garden overlooking the sea and cliffs make it a premier destination for throngs of holiday-makers in summer while on winter weekdays it is blissfully quiet.

The Anchor has two little bars with low white planked ceilings and comfortable seats around neat tables. The cottagey rooms feel particularly snug in winter with roaring fires. The walls are decorated with sea pictures and many interesting local photographs plus some fossils and shells.

They serve fresh local seafood and well-kept Palmers Ales. Barbecue food is available during the summer at weekends. The pub also offers three boutique bedrooms above the main bars with stunning sea views.

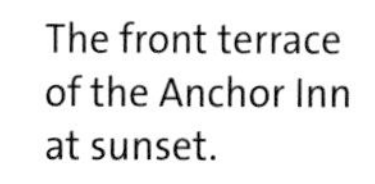

The front terrace of the Anchor Inn at sunset.

The 400-year-old Royal Standard fronts a narrow lane that runs parallel to Marine Parade.

Lyme Regis [Map 5B]
The Royal Standard

25 Marine Parade DT7 3JF Tel: 01297 442637

www.theroyalstandardlymeregis.co.uk

Lyme Regis, the last stop on our smuggling journey, is as far west as one can go in Dorset before crossing the border into Devon. The town lies in Lyme Bay, and is justifiably nicknamed 'The Pearl of Dorset'.

As part of the Jurassic Coast, it is noted for the fossils found in the cliffs and on the beaches. The harbour wall, known as 'The Cobb', features in Jane Austen's novel *Persuasion* and in *The French Lieutenant's Woman*, a novel by John Fowles, who was a Lyme resident.

Born in Devon in 1778, John (Jack) Rattenbury was a seaman and fisherman who turned to smuggling to earn a living for

The Royal Standard is the tall building in the centre of this 1825 illustration. The damage to the Cobb was a result of the November 1824 storm.

himself and his family. After thirty years involvement in the free trade, this 'Rob Roy of the West' was prevailed upon to relate his adventures and *Memoirs of a Smuggler* was published in 1837.

The sheltered suntrap courtyard at the back of the pub faces directly on to the beach with harbour views across to the famous Cobb.

Above left: There is a proper pubby bar with a good log fire.

Above right: Stained glass wall panels in the dining area tell the fascinating story of Lyme's history.

On 17 April 1801 Rattenbury married a Lyme Regis girl named Anna Partridge and they set up home in the town. The family lived in Lyme for five years and were here when Jane Austen visited in 1804. Many of Rattenbury's adventures took place in and around Weymouth and Lyme and, at this time, he would certainly have been a patron of the Royal Standard pub, facing the harbour and Cobb.

Jack Rattenbury (1778 – 1844) Lyme resident and smuggler.

Coastguards posing in front of the Watch House in the centre of this early twentieth-century photograph. The Customs House seen on the extreme left is still there although the large portico has been removed.

The sweeping arm of the Cobb shelters the small harbour from westerly gales.

Isaac Gulliver's 'White Wigs' also frequented Lyme through which they shipped masses of contraband. Gulliver died in 1824 and even two years later, the local Customs Officer seized eleven thousand gallons of spirits. This was forty percent increase on the previous year but still reckoned to be less than one-tenth of the goods that had actually been run.

On 11 May, 1844 a large fire consumed a great number of houses in Lyme amongst which was the Old Custom House, the original Cups Hotel and an ancient inn called The George where the Duke of Monmouth quartered when in Lyme. The new Custom House built in Cobb Road still stands but has lost its porch.

By 1800 Lyme was already moving away from smuggling towards its emergence as a popular watering place.

Most landed contraband was simply sneaked in under the noses of preventives, who were frequently understaffed and

handicapped by ludicrous local bylaws concerning how far their jurisdiction extended: cargoes unloaded on the Cobb could not be inspected until they had been carried half a mile to the Cobb Gate.

On the broadest part of Lyme Beach the Royal Standard has a proper pubby bar with a log fire, fine built-in high settles, local photographs and even old-fashioned ring-up tills.

There is a quieter eating area with stripped-brick and pine walls. The interior incorporates stained glass panels depicting historic events in Lyme. At the back, facing directly on to the beach is a sheltered, good-sized suntrap courtyard with own server and harbour views across to the famous Cobb.

SELECTED BIBLIOGRAPHY

M. V. Angel *In Search of Isaac Gulliver*

Eileen Hathaway *Smuggler (John Rattenbury 1778 – 1844)*

Roger Guttridge *Dorset Smugglers*

Roger Guttridge and Carol Showell *Smugglers' Trails (Pub Walks in Dorset)*

Beresford Leavens *Issac Gulliver, Le Contrebandier*

J. Meade Falkner *Moonfleet*

Geoffrey Morley *Smuggling in Hampshire and Dorset*

E. Russell Oakley *The Smugglers of Christchurch, Bournemouth and The New Forest*

Mike Powell *The Battle of Mudeford*

Allen White *18th Century Smuggling in Christchurch*